SEARCHING FOR GOD IN GODFORSAKEN TIMES AND PLACES

Reflections on the Holocaust, Racism, and Death

Hubert G. Locke

William B. Eerdmans Publishing Company
Grand Rapids, Michigan / Cambridge, U.K.

Wm. B. Eerdmans Publishing Co.
2140 Oak Industrial Drive N.E., Grand Rapids, Michigan 49505 /
P.O. Box 163, Cambridge CB3 9PU U.K.

Printed in the United States of America

08 07 06 05 04 03 7 6 5 4 3 2 1

Library of Congress Cataloging-in-Publication Data

Locke, Hubert G.
Searching for God in godforsaken times and places:
reflections on the Holocaust, racism, and death / Hubert G. Locke.
p. cm.
Includes bibliographical references.
ISBN-10: 0-8028-6084-2 / ISBN-13: 978-0-8028-6084-2 (pbk.)
1. Faith. 2. Locke, Hubert G. 3. Holocaust (Christian theology).
4. Death — Religious aspects — Christianity. 5. Racism —
Religious aspects — Christianity. I. Title.
BT774.L63 2003
231.7′6 — dc21

2003048049

www.eerdmans.com

SEARCHING FOR GOD IN GODFORSAKEN TIMES AND PLACES

In memory of my parents
Willa L. Locke (1909-1997)
Hubert H. Locke (1907-1998)

and

For my sisters
Joyce Kathleen Bridgeforth
and
Gloria Lynn Gilmer

Contents

Preface

This small volume reflects on three experiences I have confronted in my life that challenge my belief in God. Each experience represents a reality that I find either inexplicable — as in the case of the murder of six million Jews; intolerable — which is my response to the problem of race; or thoroughly menacing — as I have come to view the threat of death. Whenever I try to grapple with these three experiences — death, race, and the Holocaust or the Shoah (the preferable term for the murder of the Jews) — from the perspective of conventional Christian teaching, I find myself inclined toward skepticism regarding many of the claims and assurances of the Christian faith.

Acknowledging this does not come easy for one who would like to think of himself as an active Christian, much less for one who was ordained to the Christian ministry almost a half-century ago! I am left to wonder whether it is only now, in the seventh decade of my life, that I have summoned up the courage to confront my skepticism, or whether, as my own mortality becomes a far more real prospect, I am trying to resolve questions for which I do not have long to find answers.

One of the three experiences — that of race — has been with me all my life. I have managed for the most part not to be preoccupied by this ubiquitous fact of existence, but as I have grown older, I have become increasingly less patient with the fact that it influences so much of what takes place in the world and especially in my own society. The Shoah has been, for me, an enigma since I was a student in high school. Many of my classmates in one of Detroit's central-city high schools were Jewish, and we were completing our secondary school education immediately after the Second World War — in precisely the period during which the world was being confronted with the horrid evidence of the fate of some six million children, women, and men who were slaughtered to satisfy the sick assumptions of a small band of racial megalomaniacs.

The third experience is the more recent and the most immediately troubling, personally and theologically. It was the death of my parents — three months apart — that led me to sit down and try to compose my thoughts, first on that sad period in my life but then, as I tried to assess its meaning and implications for what I thought I believed as a "person of faith," on the other two experiences as well. I came painfully to the awareness that the three experiences had a common thread. Each — and all three together — presented questions to me that three years of graduate theological education, twelve years as pastor of a church, and, most especially, more than thirty years as a university teacher had not satisfactorily answered.

For the first time in my life I found myself trying, quietly and systematically, to allow these questions to surface in my mind and to consider possible responses that my years in the seminary, in the pulpit, and in the classroom had failed to provide. In the process, I took from my library shelves books I had not read in forty years; reading them anew was like the excitement of becoming reacquainted with old friends that one has not encountered in a long time. But just as with old friendships that one seeks to rekindle, some works provoked an almost immediate intellectual excitement, leaving me to wonder how and why I had gone for such a long time without their company, while others proved to be a sad disappointment — beyond the first spark of an old memory, there was nothing of substance with which to renew an interest.

Whether helpful or not, those tomes represent the strivings of others who have tried to come to terms with the difficult dimensions of Christian belief. They serve as useful guideposts — they save one from the folly of thinking, "I am the first to wrestle with this question" — but even those answers that resonate most with my predicament are not my answers. To my shock and relief, I came to realize that I have no other choice than to wrestle with these ancient dilemmas for myself, for, as has been the repeated discovery in the realm of Christian faith, the answers are not authentic unless they are authentic *for me.*

Arriving at this realization, I have come to recognize, is not a sign of arrogance or excessive self-centeredness. It is, instead, the simple recognition that in matters of faith nothing counts that is not a matter of personal conviction. I can explore, examine, and try to learn from the experiences that others who have wrestled with problems of doubt and faith have had, but, in the end, only my own struggle matters. My cry is that of the Psalmist: "Lord, make me to know *my* end . . ."; for, in the end, I must answer for myself as to whether I have lived a life of faithfulness to God.

Many others, I know, struggle with the same doubts, face the same uncertainties, wrestle with the same questions, and are confronted with the same threats. I have written these reflections not because they provide answers but in the hope that they will encourage others to confront the questions, and to find their own answers to them.

Finally, as I lacked the courage to ask others to read my work, I do not have the customary list of individuals to thank who were asked to read this manuscript but who should be held blameless for its contents. I do express much gratitude to my editor, Hannah Timmermans, for her diligent and insightful labors.

Chapter 1

Doubt, Uncertainty, and the Reality of Death

My mother died shortly after seven in the evening on December 16, 1997. Just before slipping into unconsciousness, she spoke briefly to my two sisters and her grandchildren who were gathered at her bedside. For each one she had a final word — a wish, a reassurance, a reminder. When she finished, she said quietly, "I am ready to go. I am at peace. I am happy in the Lord."

My mother died as she had lived for eighty-eight years — filled with an unswerving and unshakable confidence in the fundamental teachings of the Christian faith. During her adult years, she wore out at least a half-dozen Bibles from daily reading of the Scriptures. Her last Bible was as annotated extensively by her own notes, scribbled in the margins and between verses, as it was battered by her ceaseless thumbing from chapter to chapter and book to book.

Before her eyesight grew weak, she read repeatedly and systematically through the Scriptures. She was unaware of the Jewish tradition of reading through the Torah each year but she followed her own Christian version of the practice. Each word of the Bible was, to her, the word of God, a great deal of which she memorized and could recall and recite flawlessly. She died certain of its promise of the resurrection to the life which is eternal.

Her death came quickly, and although I was not at her bedside to hear her final word to me, I arrived before her last breath. For me, she had left a reminder — one that I knew all too well, for we had talked about it many times, sometimes laughingly, sometime in seriousness. I was reminded that it was her wish that I give the eulogy at her funeral. I did so because it was her wish, and, standing in the pulpit above her casket, I said what I felt most deeply about her and what I thought she would want me to say to my family and a church filled with friends for her final services. Reading over, a day or so after her burial, what I had carefully tried to compose, I realized I had spoken about her life of faith but had said nothing about her certainty in the life which is to come. I had, in fact, taken as a text for the eulogy Paul's oft-cited words to Timothy: "I have fought a good fight, I have finished my course, I have kept the faith" (2 Timothy 4:7). For reasons that escaped me at the time but that now I suspect were gnawing at me even in those painful moments, I did not recite — nor did I comment on — the words that immediately follow:

> Henceforth, there is laid up for me the crown of righteousness which the Lord, the Righteous Judge, shall give me at that day, and not to me only but to all those who love his appearing.

WHY DID I FAIL to finish Paul's affirmation? I have been plagued by this question ever since realizing what I had done — or failed to do. As agonizing as it was to stand before my mother's bier, I somehow found it easier to speak of her good life than of her hope and her longing. I knew of the former and could describe it in loving detail. Of the latter, I had only what she had — the assertions and assurances made two millennia ago and continually restated by the church ever since, that what lay before me and the congregation was not the end but part of a transition to a better world.

In the immediacy of death, those assertions and assurances are confronted by harsh, unremitting realities. My sisters, the grandchildren, and I were with my mother when she breathed her last breath. Within a half hour, her body had begun to cool. When next we saw her, the mortician had done what morticians do to try to mask the reality of death, but there was no mistaking the fact that we could view only the shell of what had once been a warm, vibrant woman who loved life almost as much as she loved God.

Following her service, we took her to the cemetery and heard the minister commit her body to the earth — "ashes to ashes, dust to dust" — knowing that an irreversible process of physical decay, only momentarily halted by the mortician, had already set in. It is not easy to speak of the hope of the resurrection when surrounded only by signs of mortality and lifelessness.

There is, in fact, the grim finality of it all. Our family is among those that devoutly observe the protocols of dying. When my mother's sickness had progressed to the stage that physicians no longer held out hope of recovery, we began a last vigil, with some from among her children and grandchildren at her bedside until she drew her last breath. We observed the traditional wake when her body was brought to the church the evening before the funeral and friends came to view her and console us. The funeral service and the burial that followed, both brief but filled with symbolism that depicted and celebrated a cherished relationship that had come to an end — everything pointed, in spite of the hymns of faith and the prayers of hope in the hereafter, to the blunt fact that life for and with our mother was over. Conversations with her, sounds of her laughter, her embraces — all this, at least in this sphere of existence, would never occur again.

In the days that followed, I found myself caught up in an aimlessness quite unlike anything I had ever experienced. Friends kept me occupied with conversation and companionship that had a calming effect for which I was grateful, but when I was alone — driving through the city or walking across campus — my mind and thoughts became transfixed on my mother's death. I would look up at the sky or, where I am fortunate to live, at a distant, snow-capped mountain and suddenly find myself comforted by a sense that my mother was at rest and in a better place. But in the next moment, I would be reminded of the scenes at her bier, of leaving her in a coffin on a quiet hillside waiting to be interred and gradually to disintegrate, in keeping with the words of the minister, "earth to earth, dust to dust."

I learned to cope with my physical aimlessness. What I was not prepared for was the extent to which I wandered, in the aftermath of my mother's death, between certainty and doubt. I felt confident that her good life in this realm had earned for her a place in whatever life there is to come. But I could not repress my doubts about that promise of immortality. How could I recite the phrase in the Creed, "I believe in . . . the resurrection of the body," when the sight of her lifeless corpse was still so fresh in my mind? What possible meaning could the words from the committal service — "in sure and certain hope of the resurrection unto eternal life" — have? How could she participate in such a life when what she was and what I remember about her, as flesh and blood, was now rapidly decaying? With a certain agony, I began to understand the cry of the father who asked Jesus to cure his son: "Lord, I believe; help my unbelief!" (Mark 9:24).

My father's death came a brief three months later. Because he required around-the-clock care, he had been moved to a nursing home a few weeks after my mother died. He passed quietly one morning: my eldest daughter, the financial administrator of the home, stopped by to greet him as she did each morning; a few hours later, he was gone. It was as if he finally came to the realization that his mate of sixty-six years had left him and he had no reason to stay behind.

In reality, my father's passing began long before my mother's death. He suffered a stroke in 1991 and for the next seven years followed a slow but inexorable descent into physical collapse and mental oblivion. It was excruciatingly painful to watch. Medically, we were told his illness was a form of dementia: brief moments of mental clarity in which he was his old self — telling a funny story or laughing at one told by someone else — were followed by long periods of confusion and almost unmanageable irrationality. Mercifully, near the end, he began to sleep for long periods, as if preparing himself for that sleep from which no one awakes.

Unlike my mother, who welcomed death as the transit to that life for which she longed, my father seemed to fear it. One could sense it in his refusal to acknowledge the death of his grandson and in the dismay with which he greeted the deaths of his older sister and younger brother — all of which took place a few years before my mother's passing. His reaction to the death of my mother was difficult to gauge; by that time his own mental deterioration had reached a stage at which it was not possible to assess his response to much of anything. All we knew was that at one moment he would break into sobs when reminded that she was gone and, moments later, call for her to bring him something to eat or drink.

My father's fear of death could be seen, most of all, in his eyes. If the eyes are, as the poets suggest, the windows to the soul, then my dad's soul was a troubled one. I was never able to gaze into my mother's eyes in the final hours before her death; she had been heavily sedated by the time I arrived at her bedside. But for several years I had occasions to watch my father awake from his prolonged periods of sleep with sheer terror in his eyes. It may only have been his momentary recognition that he was rapidly losing his grasp on this existence, but at times it was as though he had glimpsed the beyond and did not want to go there.

There were times when the apparent dullness in his eyes seemed to signal the approaching end — moments in which his eyes were so cloudy and vacant that they appeared to be cast on nothingness. Perhaps, though, they had already begun to refocus on a realm so unlike that which the living know that what we mistook as lifeless was a vision that had already begun to glimpse another domain.

Coming so quickly as they did, my parents' deaths left my two sisters and me with a certain numbness. Barely, it seemed, had we buried our mother than the family trod the same steps again — to the mortician to make final arrangements for my father, to the church for the wake and the funeral, to the cemetery where he was laid to rest beside his wife of sixty-six years. Their only grandson is buried next to them, and two of my father's brothers together with their wives and other relatives are buried close by. They lie in death as they lived, surrounded by loved ones.

"They lie . . ." — that is the poetic way we have learned to speak of the final resting place of the dead. According to Christian belief, however, it is a decidedly incorrect depiction of my parents' fate. We carried to the cemetery their physical remains; it is that which has begun the process of physical disintegration. Standing before each of their coffins, the minister committed their bodies to the earth but their souls he commended to God, to await the final resurrection, the judgment, and the life which is everlasting.

How often I have uttered the same words, standing before the open grave of someone's remains that are about to be interred. I have hoped that they were words of comfort and reassurance to those gathered at the graveside. At the very least, they are the formal pronouncements of the church, encapsulating in solemn prose the essence of the Christian hope. Now, however, hearing them uttered over my parents' bodies, I found myself listening but finding the pronouncements to be the occasion not so much for comfort as for questioning.

As to why the questions had not arisen much earlier in my life, I can only confess that prior to the death of my parents I had never been on the receiving end of the Christian message about death; that message had been mine to deliver but not to hear. I realize now what a terrible judgment that is on me and perhaps on other clergy as well who speak but who do not hear what they are saying. For the first time in my life, however, I found myself not dispensing words of comfort and reassurance but in need of receiving them. And the words I was hearing were words that raised as many — if not more — questions than they provided answers.

Christian history is strewn with the records of those who, for one reason or another, have suffered moments of great doubt or despair about their faith. I mention two illustrious examples — Martin Luther and Søren Kierkegaard (whom I shall have occasion to discuss again) — only to indicate that feeling oneself beset by questions for which conventional religious answers are inadequate is an anguish that has been the experience of far nobler Christian souls than I would ever hope to be. Nevertheless, if there is a moment and a matter about which the answers of Christian orthodoxy prove to be problematic, it is encountered most of all when one confronts death.

Reflecting on and writing about death and dying is not done easily. Some likely find it ghoulish. I find it necessary and pity those who assiduously avoid it, many of whom have never experienced death "up close and personal." To helplessly watch a loved one's labored breathing, to know that the end is near and to be conflicted by the anticipation of release and relief for the dying one but sorrow and anguish over the approaching loss, to hold one dear as the last breath leaves the body and a sudden, chilling stillness seems to surround everything — all of this is to undergo a transforming experience in one's life. Nothing, at least in the immediate aftermath, is quite the same.

A glance at the obituary column in most large-city newspapers reflects the lengths to which moderns will go to avoid the impact of death. Sometimes, the briefest biographical notation of the deceased is followed by a terse "no services," as if those who might be expected to mourn are in haste to get on with their own living. Frequently, friends and neighbors are invited to a "celebration of life" where sincere efforts to extol the virtues and recall cherished memories of the deceased often become banal recitations of anecdotes and awkward expressions of misplaced humor, designed to mask the reality of death.

In most ethnic traditions and especially those that have a strong religious core, death is accepted as the defining moment in human experience that it is. Together with birth, reaching adulthood, and marriage, death is invested with symbolic meaning in all religious communities so as to lift these events out of the ordinary and the mundane moments in life. Of all the stages of life, however, and in token of its transforming quality, death, in many ethnic communities, is uniquely given an attentiveness that none of the other moments-of-passage receive.

It is chiefly for this reason that I have regret for those who do their utmost to avoid the experience of death. It is obviously not a moment in life to wish for; seldom is it welcomed, unless it brings to a close an existence marred by prolonged illness and marked with physical pain or that which comes with the loss of mental functioning. But death is always a transforming experience for anyone who does not take steps to ignore or quickly dismiss it. The death of someone we know focuses the mind as few, if any, other events in the lives of the living can. In a moment, it can strip bare much of what we think is important and reduce our thoughts to the basic questions of life and human existence.

In the ethnic experience I know best, death is confronted with the same agonizing openness with which my kinspeople greet all of life. The deaths of my mother and my father were followed, for four days, by an emotionally exhausting round of events: a full afternoon spent with the mortician's staff, choosing a casket, selecting a shroud for my mother, ordering flowers, arranging for the grave to be opened in the family plot and, in consultation with the family minister, planning the details of the service. The day following each death, our extended family was notified and we prepared to receive relatives — who came considerable distances for the service — and friends who came throughout the days and evenings to bring food and comfort. The evening before the funeral services, my parents' bodies were brought to the church where we greeted and embraced friends around their open biers. Scriptures were read, hymns sung, and prayers offered, all in preparation for the final service the following day.

I cannot recall a black funeral in which the body of the deceased was not present. Only recently has the practice been instituted of closing the casket before the services begin. Customarily, and still in some parts of the South, not only is the casket open throughout the service, but at the service's close the family is led forward for a final farewell. All of this, even the more modern alterations, may strike many as macabre. For me, as for most black people who still follow the custom, it is an utterly emptying experience. By the time we took my parents' bodies to their final resting place, my heart literally ached but I was drained of tears. I had only my sadness and my nagging doubt with which to deal.

That doubt was not lessened by my realization, for the first time, of how diffuse and diverse the biblical record is regarding immortality. It was not that I was unaware of the many not-quite-consistent passages regarding eternal life in the Scriptures; it was, rather, that in the aftermath of facing mortality in such a direct and immediate way, I found myself with the motivation to pay closer attention to them. Part of what I came to realize was that if one seeks consistency in the biblical narratives, one is bound to be disappointed.

One can begin with Job's ringing declaration: "For I know that my Redeemer liveth, and that he shall stand at the latter day upon the earth: / And though after my skin worms destroy this body, yet in my flesh shall I see God" (Job 19:25-26). Here is the affirmation of a man who, it can also be noted, had more than ample reason to doubt traditional teachings about the goodness of God, but who nevertheless proclaims his conviction that — in spite of the physical decay of the body after death — he will see God in the flesh.

There is likely no more disputed text in all of Scripture (regarding what the Hebrew text actually says or means) than this verse. The textual disputes, however, do not overcome the blunt assertion of Job; it is one of the foundational statements of belief in the resurrection of the body to be found in the Bible. When placed alongside the statements of Paul about the afterlife, however, a different view of immortality emerges. In his Corinthian letter, Paul speaks of what he terms "a mystery":

> We will all be changed . . . for this perishable nature must put on the imperishable, and this mortal nature must put on immortality. [When this happens], then shall come to pass the saying that is written:

"Death is swallowed up in victory." O death, where is thy sting? O grave, where is thy victory? (1 Corinthians 15:52-55)

This passage (to which we will return in Chapter Seven) is preceded by a rather lengthy discussion by Paul of the topics of resurrection and immortality. It is a lengthy and complicated presentation on Paul's part; essentially he argues that the resurrection of Jesus is at the heart of the Christian message, that the significance of Jesus' resurrection lies, among other things, in the fact that, in contrast to the first man Adam who is a symbol of human mortality, Jesus is a sign of the immortality that all may achieve. There follows a brief description of what the commentaries on this passage call "the eschatological drama" and then a discussion of the nature of the bodily resurrection, culminating in the passage cited above.

Clearly, Paul's expectation is not that of Job. Paul does not anticipate a resuscitation of the human body but the resurrection of an entirely new and different substance or being — what is "sown" as "perishable, weak, and physical" will be raised as "imperishable, powerful and spiritual." In direct contrast to Job, in fact, Paul flatly asserts that "flesh and blood cannot inherit the kingdom of God" (15:50).

The sayings of Jesus about the next life present yet more differences. There is, on the one hand, his promise to one of the thieves crucified with him that the thief would join Jesus in paradise, as well as the story of Dives and Lazarus (Luke 16:19-31), which also suggests that mortals are judged by God immediately upon death and sent to hell or paradise accordingly. But when placed alongside Jesus' depiction of the Great Judgment in Matthew's Gospel (Matthew 25:31-46), both the Dives-Lazarus story and the crucifixion account would seem to imply some immediate stage or realm in the afterlife where souls have been already judged, in contrast to the idea of lying in death, awaiting a final judgment.

Finally, there are the majestically confusing passages of the Apocalypse which have been the source of so much doctrinal controversy in the life of the church. John writes of not one but two resurrections — the first for martyrs of the faith, the second for the rest of the dead. John depicts a place of punishment in which some of the dead reside, suggesting parallels with the Dives-Lazarus and crucifixion stories, but he also envisions a final judgment, the renovation or transformation of the existing universe, and the emergence of "a new heaven and a new earth." It is from the new heaven that John glimpses the holy city — the "new Jerusalem" — where the faithful live in the presence of God and where "there is no more death" (Revelation 21:1-4).

One senses, in all these not-quite-consistent accounts, the effort to say a few things consistently. One is the belief in an existence or a realm beyond this world. On this, all of the stories agree; they might differ regarding its shape, form, and substance, but not its reality. Such is their confidence about the life which is to come, in fact, that they affirm its existence under the most agonizing of circumstances; neither Job nor Jesus is enjoying the comfort of armchair reflection when he speaks of immortality. Job is in the midst of a seemingly endless series of personal catastrophes when he declares his certainty about seeing God while Jesus is suffering the agony of his execution when he commits his spirit to God. It is possible, of course, to dismiss these affirmations as the delusional cries of those who are under stressful circumstances. But stress can produce the opposite result as well; it is often under conditions of strain and distress that one sees most clearly what is true and important about life — in this case, that it is not bound by the limitations of this mortal realm or, as the philosophers and theologians would put it, by the threat of non-being.

The second affirmation that each of these narratives makes is a moral one. They declare that we will all confront the obligation to answer for our conduct in this life. This is at the heart of the story of Dives and Lazarus but it is also the primary reason for Job's lament; he does not understand why he should be visited with so many afflictions and hardships since he has tried, he believes, to live his life by rules of decency and responsibility. Jesus, too, feels he has finished the work God sent him to do and for this very reason wonders why God has forsaken him. Paul is quite convinced that apart from the necessity of accounting for our earthly deeds, there is no reason we should not "eat, drink, and be merry, for tomorrow we die" (1 Corinthians 15:32). And John's Apocalypse is the most explicit: he recites, several times over, a list of offenses and offenders who will be excluded from the bliss of the holy city because of their behavior in this life, while he lauds those who have been the "witnesses of Jesus" and thereby earned the right to the tree of life.

One senses also that there was simply not a great deal of preoccupation with the problem of consistency in these narratives, much less with the problem of scientific credibility. These are stories, events, and declarations that are recited to make a moral point or to express a spiritual truth. From the stories surrounding Jesus' resurrection, it is clear that there was no greater group of skeptics than Jesus' own disciples — and not just Thomas but those who were unable to recognize him because they were so unprepared for the resurrection event. It is, perhaps, when one lets go of the urge to understand death and immortality according to the canons of human reason, and instead seeks to grasp their moral and spiritual meaning, that one finds the true meaning of salvation and redemption.

MY MOTHER'S DEATH and burial, a week before Christmas, and that of my father, a few days before Easter, are forever framed in my mind by these two great festivals of the Christian year. It was especially difficult to part with them just prior to holidays that they both looked forward to and that were always occasions of great joy and celebration in our family. Christmas and Easter have both become secular events in modern society but they are first and foremost holy days that speak to two powerful truths in the Christian world. The first is easiest to grasp and celebrates something that Christians acclaim together with all the earth's inhabitants: the joy and excitement of birth and new life, the manifestation of innocence, the unending possibilities that can be contemplated for the newborn, with all the promise the birth presents for growth and achievement. Easter proclaims a truth that is more difficult to accept, although its hope is of the greater moment. Easter affirms, as Karl Barth declares, that "death is not the last reality; it is a reality limited by God."[1] If Christmas celebrates the most natural and ordinary of human experiences — the birth of a child — then Easter declares that the most unordinary and trans-natural event has also taken place in our earthly realm, and that because of it, we have no need to fear death as the end of everything. Christmas marks the beginning of life with all of its possibilities; Easter points to the defeat of death and the promise of an even more abundant existence.

Taken together, these two great Christian festivals surround our lives with promise and expectation. Both are celebrations that have taken on as much secular significance as religious meaning, but it is the religious meaning and message that ought to be paramount. It is the religious meaning, however, that gives me pause, for somehow the certainty with which I can affirm the significance of the birth of a child does not carry over into the reality I confront when I am faced with death, especially the death of loved ones. It is relatively easy to think that God is somehow revealed in the trustful, innocent face of a newborn babe. It becomes infinitely more difficult, at least for me, to see God and to be convinced of the promise of immortality when staring into an open grave.

1. Richard R. Niebuhr, *Resurrection and Historical Reason* (New York: Scribners, 1957), p. 33.

Chapter 2

On the Nature of Doubt . . .

Except for those who suffer from self-delusion, most of us live our lives suspended between certainty and doubt. If we are among the fortunate who have known the nurture of loving parents, the affection of a mate, the devotion of children, and the joy of close friends, we have a sense of that security which lies in the knowledge that we are loved and esteemed by those dear to us. But this certainty is not unalloyed. A father's anger, a mother's anguish, a spouse's inattention or indifference, a son's or daughter's rebellion, and we wonder, even if momentarily, if the sureness we feel is as rooted as we think or wish.

There are other spheres of our lives in which the personal relationship may be far less intimate or even nonexistent but there is nonetheless a certainty we take for granted. We drive to and from work, run errands, shop, and pursue leisure activities secure in the belief that the engineers who designed the bridges and freeway spans we cross and the construction crews who built them were competent purveyors of their crafts. We turn on the faucets in our homes or sip from the water coolers at the office or factory sufficiently confident that those unknown persons who manage municipal watersheds, monitor the water's purity, and secure its transmission against tampering or terrorism have all done their tasks responsibly that we do not give it a second thought.

These days an unquestioning confidence in physicians may be somewhat diminished from that of earlier times, but here as well our reliance on doctors' competence is sufficient for us to take their judgments as decisive, even if those judgments move us to seek a second opinion. We are sure that our well-being rests, in large measure, on their medical expertise; it is our faith in a physician's professional knowledge and skill that is at the heart of the doctor-patient relationship. It is our sense of certainty that others whom we encounter know what they are doing and will do it well — the bus driver who will transport us safely to our destination, the butcher who will not sell us tainted meat, the chef at the restaurant who studiously avoids the danger of food poisoning, the financial planner who will not give us erroneous tax advice, or countless others whom we've never met or will never see but on whom our safety and well-being depends, such as airplane pilots — that makes possible our ability to go about our daily chores without being in a constant state of panic.

Just as with intimate relationships, however, the public and professional facets of our lives can be clouded by doubt and disappointment. In both realms, the unexpected happens or the abnormal occurs: We hear of a bridge collapse or a plane crash due to pilot error, we read of a medical malpractice suit or an accountant who diverts a client's funds for personal use, and suddenly we find ourselves feeling less certain about our own security than we might wish. We find ourselves, in such moments, reminded that life, in spite of endless efforts to make our existence as secure as possible, is unpredictable.

If portions of our lives are spent suspended between doubt and certainty, we also devote much of our living to attempts at decreasing the arena of doubt and expanding the spheres of certitude. We do so in ways that can be frivolous, practical, or ludicrous. Some people spend long hours in line at box offices in order to make certain they can purchase choice seats at some sporting or musical event. Most of us buy health and life insurance to hedge against the uncertainties of illness and the certainty of death. Then there are those who arrange to have their bodies frozen when they die, in a feeble attempt to deny the inevitableness of life's end.

We try to fill our lives with certainty — with whatever it is on which we think we can depend — but still death gives rise to our ultimate doubts. Most of us cringe at the thought of death as the end of everything. Something within most if not all of us longs to think of or to envision an existence beyond this earthly realm. That longing has been encouraged and reinforced as a virtually universal fact of human existence. Every culture and society, from earliest recorded history to the present, has in some fashion or other imagined an afterlife, and those imaginings have been depicted in art, expressed in literature and music, and chiseled in stone down through the ages. Where a written record is absent, they have been transmitted in countless oral traditions. It is especially in a society's religious instincts that the visions of life beyond death are likely to be preserved.

In the first few days after my mother's death, I found myself wondering whether the notion of an afterlife might be just that — part of the elaborate mental superstructure we erect over the harsh reality of life's end in order to mask its finality. Is belief in an afterlife simply a way of soothing the stark grimness of death and the certainty of decay? Granted the virtual universality of belief in some form of existence after this life, might not the religious ideas of immortality be a consoling but, in the final analysis, unconvincing spiritual attempt to overcome a physical reality that cannot be denied?

For an ordained minister who, for over a dozen years while in an active pastorate, conducted countless funeral services and consoled many grieving families, such thoughts were immensely disturbing. Somehow, I felt I dishonored my mother's unquenchable faith and the sacredness of her memory — not to mention my own pastoral calling — by allowing such doubts to enter my mind. But they could not be easily shaken! Her death left an emptiness in my life and world that I knew would never again be filled. The tearful scenes of her final moments and the funereal aftermath were still strong in my mind's eye. They formed an unshakable image of a door that had been closed in my life that would never reopen, no matter how much I believed, how hard I prayed, or how intensely I might wish otherwise.

Doubt is not a new experience for me, although the death of my parents gave rise to uncertainties I had not experienced before. Doubt, in fact, has always been a part of my existence — so much so that I have always marveled at people who seem to be cocksure of everything. My own doubts have centered largely on myself; often they have had to do with my ability to successfully complete a complicated task or deal with a difficult personal relationship. Doubts have surfaced especially in relation to my career and whether I would meet its demands and live up to others' expectations. My doubts have been almost at one with my career, for I have pursued a vocation in which doubt is virtually an occupational prerequisite.

I was ordained over forty years ago, but I have spent most of the past four decades in the academy rather than in the pulpit. It has been a good professional life to pursue, with its own satisfactions and rewards. Now retired from a university professorship, I can both recognize and appreciate how much my habits of thought and, correspondingly, my inclinations to doubt have been shaped by the pervasive skepticism of the university world. Universities are in the business of producing and transmitting knowledge of all sorts and descriptions — about the earth and the atmosphere, about continents and their formation, about the myriad forms of life on this planet, about the human body, the workings of the mind, the associations we form, the institutions we create, and how we behave in groups. Much of what we do and enjoy in modern life is based upon the reliability of this knowledge — a reliability that is established by its having been repeatedly and continually questioned, tested, and found to be dependable.

Questioning is a way of life in the university. Asking what things are and why they appear as they do is the elemental starting point of scientific inquiry. Nothing is accepted as fact unless it can be subjected to the most rigorous scrutiny and until it is held up to a relentless barrage of skeptical examination. Generally, theories that cannot undergo such searching scrutiny do not fare well in scholarly circles.

As important to our lives as the discoveries that have emerged from this tough-minded, empirical process are, few of them satisfy the deepest human longings or answer the most troublesome questions of our existence. Medical science enables us to live longer, the marvels of engineering enable us to build higher and travel faster, and the astonishing developments in communications technology increase the forms and the rapidity with which we can interact with one another. But answers to questions about what constitutes a good life (when it is measured other than by acquisitions) remain elusive for most people. And answers about death — whether it has a spiritual meaning as well as a physical inescapability or whether it is the end of all that there is, for example — are not generated by the best of the university's intellectual efforts.

Even though it may not have all the answers to the questions of human existence, however, the inquiring stance that is so endemic to university life tends to make its habitués skeptical of the easy or authoritative affirmations of those who claim to have the answers to all of life's riddles. The assertions and assurances that are put forth by those who presume to have the solutions to life's questions are viewed with a disquiet that arises from an unwillingness to take seriously anything that cannot itself be questioned. The unease is heightened whenever it involves or requires trusting in someone else's version of reality.

All of this poses immense difficulty for anyone for whom faith is as much a part of life as are reason and skepticism. It is not that faith and reason are incompatible. Faith is not blind belief in the irrational or the impossible — such would be a denial of the very essence we are taught that we have been given as God's creation. A God who makes humans with the capacity to question and doubt surely does not turn around and ask or demand that we suspend that capacity in the face of those events or moments that cause us to wonder or to be uncertain. The difficulty stems from the fact that what we know with the greatest degree of confidence is what we can see and touch or taste and smell — that which comes to us directly and unmistakably through our physical senses. We recognize, of course, that even in this physical realm we are capable of being deceived. Not everything is as it appears or presents itself to us. How much greater then is our unsureness about assertions we are asked to accept or appeals for our trust that come from sources we cannot experience directly. And if the assertions or appeals seem to run counter to what we experience — as the affirmations of eternal life do in the face of bodily decay — then the temptation to doubt grows stronger yet.

And yet we also recognize that not everything in which we have confidence is based upon our physical senses or our direct experience. In fact, what is of greatest importance to us in life often lies beyond the realm of the senses. My remaining family is now scattered all across the United States and our contact is most frequently by phone, but that does not diminish the affection that connects us to one another. I treasure many deep and lasting relationships with friends although we also are separated by long distances from one another. Months may pass when we are not in touch, but those friendships are enduring.

To cite another example: Now that I am retired, I am financially dependent on people I have never met who manage an effort I know only from documents I receive and read. But those people and that effort result in an allotment which comes with regularity each month and which I have every confidence will continue to do so for as long as I live. I pause to wonder if there is any essential difference between the reliance I am asked to have in the promise of immortality and that which I have that the pledge my retirement fund makes will also be fulfilled? In both cases I have only documents on which to rely. My future financial well-being in this world is a matter of which I am confident because I can read the quarterly reports of those to whom I have entrusted my resources — people I have never seen but on whom my well-being depends. Does this differ from the trust I am asked to have in the promise of a life beyond this realm of which I read in the Scriptures? What is the difference between depending on the reliability of pension fund managers whom I have never seen but whose reports and reassurances I read and trusting the witness of those witnesses whose accounts I read in Holy Writ? Only one thing is for certain: in the latter instance, the stakes are a great deal higher.

The experience of death brings all of this to the fore in an unmistakable way. Our physical senses tell us in undeniable ways that a radical, wrenching separation has occurred — breath has ceased, life has been severed from the body, and a transformation has begun that will result in the gradual decay and decomposition of the human form. We may be deceived in other aspects of our experience but here there is no deception. What we experience when we confront death is a reality that is certain and changeless.

DOUBT, IN SOME RESPECTS, is a healthy attitude. The fact that I am disinclined to believe the odometer reading in a used car that I might be inclined to purchase can save me from being duped or disappointed in the car's subsequent performance. My distrust in my ability to swim long distances undoubtedly saves me from risking my life in some foolish or ill-considered moment. When doubt serves as a caution, it inclines us toward prudence by inviting us to think and consider lest we act unwisely. Doubt may also serve as an incentive — a spur to examine more intensely or inquire into matters at greater length than we otherwise might. My misgiving about the accuracy of a restaurant bill can cause me to look at each charge carefully. A chronological gap in the resumé of someone I am considering for a job moves me to check out the person's background with an especial thoroughness. In these and many other ways, to be unsure is to avoid gullibility and taking for granted matters that warrant more careful consideration.

It is not the positive features of doubt that are troubling but, rather, doubt's debilitating features. Self-doubt — doubt about the ability to handle a situation or about whether one has the skills necessary to accomplish a certain task — can motivate a person to self-improvement but can also traumatize and incapacitate to such an extent that one is unable to do anything. Doubting the intentions or motives of others can become dysfunctional if it makes one so innately suspicious of people that trust and openness are difficult to muster.

As important to our well-being as these areas of our lives are, they pale in significance to the arena that faith encompasses, making ever more vexatious the doubt that can threaten our faith. Whatever else may be said, faith in God has to do with things that matter ultimately. Faith is not about life's trivia. Whenever and wherever questions of faith are raised, they concern our deepest, most critical concerns. Accordingly, to be uncertain about matters of faith is to lose confidence in those very foundations on which persons of faith erect their existence. Uncertainty in the arena of faith for the person of faith is to lose one's mooring and to find oneself cast adrift in life without those points or frames of reference which guide one's daily steps. It is no wonder that there is such a short spiritual distance between doubt and despair.

It is also little wonder that many people opt for what clearly is a far easier course — to accept at face value the orthodox answers that the church gives to the life-and-death questions of human existence. These are the believers who find it unnecessary, if not heretical, to agonize over questions of faith when the answers are all given in Scripture or in the creeds or by the infallible pronouncements of some spiritual authority — be it pope or pastor. What goes unrecognized by such persons is the degree to which doubt has helped to form the church's most enduring teachings. It has been those who first have wrestled with doubt and uncertainty who have produced the convictions that are to be found in the classic statements of Christian belief that are part of the rich record of Christian thought and reflection.

It becomes evident, in fact, when one surveys the two millennia of Christian thought, that doubt is a very common — one might almost say essential — Christian virtue! To claim such is not to try crudely to make a virtue out of necessity. It is, rather, to understand that virtually since its inception, Christianity has had among its followers those who, at some point, were doubtful about its claims and its assertions. And for those who see Scripture as the infallible record of Christian truth, it should be of more than passing interest that it is the Christian Scriptures that are replete with the experiences of doubters.

From a philosophical perspective, no one has better enabled us to understand the essentially positive features of doubt than Josiah Royce, who declares, "the soul that never has doubted does not know whether it believes. . . ." Royce charts four "great ages of doubt," as he terms them, ages that begin with the Greeks, include a "sterner age of doubt [that] brought about the beginnings of Christian thought," and culminate in the writings that span the period between the death of Spinoza (1677) and the publication of Immanuel Kant's *Critique of Pure Reason* (1781). Royce sees these "fruitful periods" in history as having driven thinkers "from the study of nature to the study first of human reason, then of human conscience, then of all the human heart and soul, and meanwhile cleared the way for those triumphs of the spirit over great evils. . . ." He concludes:

> Despise not doubting; it is often the best service thinking men can render to their age. Condemn it not; it is often the truest piety. . . . Doubt is never the proper end of thinking, but it is a good beginning. The wealth of truth which our life, our age, our civilization, our religion, our own hearts may contain, is not quite our property until we have won it. And we can win it only when we have first doubted the superficial forms in which at the outset it presents itself to our apprehension.[1]

Doubt, then, is not an act of disrespect or willful arrogance. Much less is it a sign of the cynical attitude toward the possibility of attaining any truth which permeated the thought of the Greek academy that took Skepticism as its defining characteristic. Neither is doubt a matter of faithlessness. Rather, as Paul Tillich so cogently suggests, doubt is that deeply felt sense of insecurity that is inevitably present in every act of commitment. Anyone who has

1. Josiah Royce, *The Spirit of Modern Philosophy* (New York: George Braziller, 1955), pp. 71-72.

ever been in love knows exactly what Tillich calls this "existential doubt." It is the insecurity we feel in the very moment that we let go of all cautions and restraints and acknowledge that we have become captive of the object of our affections. There is, in such a moment, an undertow of agony that wonders what will happen if our love is not returned — if, as the romantics would say, it goes unrequited — or even worse, if we give our heart to someone who grasps it eagerly only to reject it and us later. We recognize painfully that in every act of loving someone we put ourselves at risk, that we give up the security we enjoy when we have only ourselves to think of, and become wholly dependent on another for our sense of satisfaction and well-being.

The religious doubter — who dares to look in the face of God and ask questions — knows this same sense of insecurity and risk. It is to give oneself wholly to God knowing that in the very act and moment of doing so, we have taken upon ourselves the risk that accompanies every commitment we make in this life. It means that we must still be prepared for life's cruelties and disappointments without any absolute assurances or guarantees, with only trust that the One to whom we have given ourselves will keep faith with us. The Christian doubter is convinced, after weighing all the arguments and evidence against the act of committing one's self to God, that such trust is not misplaced.

Set over against all my doubts and disquiet regarding traditional Christian teachings about immortality is the ringing declaration of Paul in his second letter to Timothy: "for I know whom I have believed, and am persuaded that he is able to keep that which I have committed to him until the Day [of Judgment]" (1:12). In his letter to the Corinthian Christians, Paul stated that we mortals are capable of only partial knowledge and that even the partial knowledge we think we possess can prove to be ephemeral. Here in Second Timothy, however, there is no hint of hesitation or lack of confidence. This is an affirmation of faith par excellence. Perhaps it is such because Paul is older — nearer, in fact, the end of his life when he has sorted out his priorities from peripheral matters — and therefore able to speak with unflagging certainty about what is central in his life. Or it may be that Paul's trust and confidence in his Lord is of an entirely different kind and substance than the knowledge one might have of everyday events and relationships.

Whatever its source in Paul's life, this was the same confidence with which my mother drew her last breath. It is the confidence I seek and toward which I pray I may move with each of life's passing years.

Chapter 3

. . . and the Character of Certainty

Some nineteen hundred years after Paul's assertion that "I know whom I have believed," Simone Weil is said to have declared that "in what concerns divine things, belief is not appropriate. Only certainty will do. Anything less than certainty is unworthy of God."

In the intervening centuries, countless believers have proclaimed similar convictions. They have warned against halfhearted or unsteady affirmations of belief and denounced those whose faith is not firm, echoing the sentiment of James, Jesus' brother, that the person who asks of God but is doubtful "is like a wave of the sea that is driven and tossed by the wind." Such a person, James states in his epistle, is "double-minded" (literally, "two-souled"), "unstable in everything," and "must not suppose he will receive anything from the Lord" (1:6-8).

There is a considerable body of Christian literature that levels a harsh judgment against those who are less than sure about their religious beliefs; no room is left in the company of Christian believers for those who are hesitant or still struggle with questions about the Christian message and its assertions. Such views leave one asking whether certainty about the claims of that message is an absolute requirement for Christian discipleship. Can one be a follower of Christ and yet be unsure of some of the claims made in his name?

In one respect it is not difficult to understand why certainty is such an insistent demand in some quarters of the Christian community and why, for many Christians, certainty has such bedrock appeal. If religion has to do with those questions in life that are of greatest significance — with who we are and why we exist and what is our destiny — and if, for Christians, the gospel provides answers to these questions, then it follows that these are matters about which one should not be halfhearted. Simone Weil's declaration makes good sense; if our concern is with things divine — things that are eternal and transcendent — then such matters are not of casual interest or for tepid commitment.

At the same time and as it has become commonplace to observe, we live in a world filled with uncertainties — the security of one's job, the stability of the stock market, one's health, even (as we Americans have discovered to our dismay) the outcome of presidential elections! Wherever we turn, those supports or assurances on which we hope we can rely are apt to fail us. In such an insecure environment, a yearning for that which is absolutely dependable and unshakable has an especial attraction.

Certainty denotes that which is definite, fixed, and clearly established. In stark contrast to the insecurity and hesitation that lie behind doubt, certainty conveys a sense of sureness and confidence that overcomes any indecisiveness or vacillation toward which one might be inclined. Precisely because religious faith has to do with those questions that are — or should be — of ultimate importance, it is not surprising that many Christians seek a spiritual certainty that is, in every respect, absolutely and utterly dependable. They wish to be assured that their confidence in the claims of Christianity is not misplaced, and that confidence is bolstered by the certainty with which they hold their doctrinal convictions.

This desire for certainty in one's beliefs seems especially compelling within conservative wings of Christianity where the emphasis on salvation grounded in a personal relationship with Jesus is paramount. If salvation and the future depend on establishing a vital, individual relationship with the One sent by God as a sacrifice for the sins of humankind, then everything turns not on being able to understand the future or having reliable answers to life's riddles but on the depth and steadfastness of an individual's relationship with Jesus Christ. Whatever the question, for the conservative believer the answer is found in faith in Jesus whom one accepts as personal Savior and therefore as all that is needed to secure one's future, both in this life and that which is to come.

Nowhere is this confidence better expressed than in the black spiritual in which the soloist asks a series of questions — "Have you got true religion? Have you been baptized? Does your soul feel happy?" — and the congregation sings out in answer to each query: "Certainly, Lord!" Here the response is meant not only as a positive answer to the soloist's questions; it is also an affirmation of confidence that one has done all the right things where Christian faithfulness is concerned and can therefore rest secure in the knowledge that one's destiny is in the hands of God's anointed.

I QUIETLY LONG for the faith of my mother, but I know that I cannot simply appropriate her convictions and make them my own. For better or worse, I am on my own and must wrestle with the demands of the gospel and my own inner quandaries, in the hope that I, too, can find firm ground for my faith. This very formulation of what it is that I seek leads me to ask exactly what it is that the gospel demands of me. Am I asked to accept a personal relationship with Jesus as my Savior? Have James and Weil set too high a price on faith? Am I and are we obligated to have an unwavering level of certitude before we can be considered Christians? If so, of what must we be certain? Must we be certain of what various segments of the church have taught, or of the teachings of its Lord, or of the strength of our own convictions?

The business of accepting Jesus as my personal savior — as fervent evangelicals insist one must do — has always bothered me. It reduces the relationship to a one-way affair in which the believer passively embraces the idea that Jesus personally assures deliverance from God's wrath or preservation from everlasting destruction. It requires no effort on the believer's part other than to acknowledge this belief and affirm its acceptance. It turns redemption into a painless, low-cost spiritual transaction captured accurately by the old evangelical hymn "Jesus Paid It All."

The principal problem with this notion is that it has absolutely no basis in Scripture. The New Testament makes repeatedly clear, in the relatively limited number of references it makes to Jesus as Savior, that he has been sent by God to be savior of the world. There is a disagreement of long-standing between various sectors of Christian belief as to whether Jesus saves the world by saving individuals from the world's evil environs or whether he sought to redeem the whole of God's creation. Under either circumstance, reducing the divine effort to an atomistic, personal process makes too little of the work of Christ and too much of the significance of us mortals. In the end, the Jesus-as-personal-savior appeal strikes me as a typically American notion that happens to fit, theologically, with the exaggerated ideas of individual self-importance that are so prominent in popular American sentiment.

But the certainty demanded by those who call for an unwavering faith seems excessive as well. This certainty, too, does not seem wholly consistent with the record of Scripture. The latter contains far too many stories of persons who were not fully convinced of the accounts they were given about Jesus or who wanted to ask questions about what they heard. Those stories — of the man who asked Jesus to cure his son of what appears to be a case of epilepsy, of not only Thomas but apparently the bulk of the disciples who were skeptical of the resurrection accounts — have to be in Scripture for a reason! Clearly, they are not told to provide an occasion for condemning the hesitant and uncertain. They were remembered and recorded because they reflect the most human of inclinations — to want to find out all that we can and to have as much sound reason as possible before committing ourselves to that which is extraordinary.

What, then, is required or demanded of me before I can be considered a Christian? The early church made the matter intensely simple. The earliest confessional obligation we know of is the simple declaration that "Jesus is Lord." Long before the more elaborate creedal formulations were composed, those who wished to be followers of Jesus acknowledged and affirmed him to be their Lord, the one whose cause they wished to serve and whose life they wished to emulate.

As to Jesus' cause, we need have no doubt as to what that was. He proclaimed it at the very outset of his ministry and pursued it with unwavering determination until his death. He believed that he was guided by God "to preach good news to the poor, to heal the brokenhearted, to proclaim deliverance to the captives and the recovery of sight to the blind, to set at liberty those that are bruised, and to proclaim the acceptable year of the Lord" (Luke 4:18-19). He taught that those who became his disciples and who set about the same tasks in his service would help usher in the reign of the kingdom of God. The story of how this profoundly simple acknowledgment of a clearly stated mission became recast, over the centuries, into the manifold creeds, the various theologies, the confessions, crusades, doctrines, dogmas, and liturgies, the denominational variations, and all the other elements that make up Christendom is part and parcel of the history of Western civilization for the past two millennia. In many (but not all!) respects, it is a rich and wonderful history, but it ought not be allowed to overwhelm the simple fact that Christian discipleship was at the outset and remains two millennia later fundamentally a matter of commitment to Jesus as Lord.

Examining this commitment may lead to an understanding of what is the certainty we seek in our faith or, failing this, of what certainty is possible where Christian belief is concerned. Søren Kierkegaard, the Danish writer who has been called the greatest Protestant Christian of the nineteenth century, put it best. He asks, can one learn from history anything about Christ? "No," Kierkegaard answers. "Why not? Because we can 'know' nothing at all about 'Christ.' He is the paradox, the object of faith, existing only for faith . . . about Him nothing can be known, He can only be believed."[1]

Kierkegaard's assertion is a radical pronouncement, to say the least! It is a

1. In Robert Bretall, *A Kierkegaard Anthology* (Princeton, N.J.: Princeton University Press, 1951), p. 388.

direct challenge to our modern way of thinking — a denial that we can have the kind of awareness or recognition or experience of Christ that we have concerning objects or issues in all other realms of our existence. Much less, if this assertion of Kierkegaard is taken seriously, can we be convinced or have the certainty about Christ that we seek in so many other areas of our life. Here is a staunch rebuke both to those who seek the comfort and security of a personal savior and to those who want the assurance that comes from well-reasoned reflection. Instead, Kierkegaard says, Christ can only be believed. Certainty is to be found neither in knowledge, as we understand the process of knowing, nor in some personal encounter or relationship, such as we might have with family, a friend, or a loved one. Certainty, instead, is the outcome of the act of faith. It is the end to which one comes who can say with Paul, "I know whom I have believed. . . ."

Such is the judgment of a man of whom it is said that he "made the discovery that one must 'find a truth which is true for *me* — the idea for which I can live and die.'" And, as Robert Bretall goes on to relate in his Kierkegaard anthology, "When S[øren] K[ierkegaard] wrote these words in his *Journal* he already suspected what his 'idea' was, and before long he had become certain. The idea was Christianity; and his one thought was 'what it means to be a Christian.'"[2]

Such thinking cannot help but bring us up short, for it is such a radical departure from the way we normally go about making assessments and judgments in our everyday world. When I think about those things of which I want to be certain, they are also the matters for which I have solid, reliable ways of confirming or, at least, of being confident. If I look at a map in order to choose the best route from Seattle to San Antonio, I may be certain that what cartographers have reduced to lines on a paper is an accurate depiction of the routes between the two cities. Or, if I choose in the course of a day to utilize any one of the myriad technologies that we moderns enjoy, I am certain that they will perform — except for the occasional malfunction — the tasks I expect: a flick of a switch produces light or heat, the turn of a handle results in a flow of water, the push of buttons and I can hear the voice of my daughter, sister, or friend. It is certainty in the sense of predictability, dependability, and reliability that I seek and expect, and that is what I receive from the realm of technology that pervades so much of my world and existence.

In matters religious, however, Kierkegaard would have me understand that I have moved into a realm of a different order. I may long for the same kind of certainty about immortality that I expect when I read a map or turn

2. Bretall, *Kierkegaard Anthology*, p. xx.

on a switch; I may wish to have the same sort of assurance about my ultimate life destiny that my bank statement gives me about my financial circumstances. But I must recognize that in thinking about immortality or most other questions of religious or spiritual moment, I have entered a sphere that is much more akin to those moments in which I enjoy the beauty of a sunset, the warmth of a cherished memory, or the thought of a very special relationship. In none of these instances can I enjoy a technologically dependable certainty — I know, scientifically, that the sun doesn't "set," I recognize that cherished memories become embellished with the passing of time, and what I believe to be a special relationship may not be as secure as I think or would like. But I am able to gain a certainty in these experiences that parallels the confidence I have in those areas of life in which I find reliability and dependability in the wonders of technology. That certainty comes when I risk taking what Kierkegaard termed "the leap," which is the act of faith — faith in the trustworthiness of the ones whom I cherish and in the One who is Jesus the Lord.

What are the certainties about this life and the next that I may have if I affirm Jesus as Lord and commit myself to his discipleship? I may be certain that this life is about good and not evil, that its meaning is to be found in giving, not in getting, that, in Paul's words, the things that are "true, honorable, just, pure, lovely, and gracious" are the things that ultimately matter in life and that are worthy of my attempts to emulate. Of all these things I can be certain because they are what Jesus taught and did and because, if I look around me, these are the characteristics and qualities of life I most admire in others. But, from the perspective of faith, this is the easy part. The difficulty comes when I turn to the question of certainty about the life which is to come.

Questions about immortality are difficult primarily because I want to cling to the forms of knowing and certitude that have become hallmarks of the modern era. In the so-called developed world, we enjoy a longevity, an ease of travel and communication, and all sorts of conveniences in large measure because we employ the knowledge that comes from scientific investigation and its technical application. I sometimes feel the need to think and reflect in a similar fashion regarding the eternal verities. But slowly I come to the realization that such thinking will not work precisely because, as Kierkegaard understood, "it subjects the self-revelation of the infinite God to finite human standards."[3]

Philosophers and theologians, in one fashion or another, have insisted on

3. In Bretall, *Kierkegaard Anthology*, p. xxiii.

this basic truism for ages. The New Testament scholar Rudolf Bultmann and the philosopher Martin Heidegger both speak of the creature who is a self "blindly subject to affections or moods, the causes of which it cannot specify. . . . This creature's despair is due to [the] refusal to accept the knowledge of his limitedness . . . and to efforts to acquire mastery over his destiny." Such a person tries "to reduce the future to a certainty" that is not possible to grasp or gain, for, as Bultmann asserts, "the Word of Salvation comes from the other side of all human language and experience."[4]

THUS HAVE MANY of the best Christian thinkers made the case for the revelation of God in the life and work of Jesus as the path to a true knowledge of God and for faith as the only means by which that knowledge of God is apprehended. This is the understanding on which I was raised as a youth and from which I rebelled because of the fundamentalist frames in which it was presented. Now that I am much older, I find myself drawn again to this basic understanding — without its fundamentalist forms. I long ago discovered that being a follower of Christ does not oblige one to become weighted down with the centuries of accretive utterances that have been made in his name. Rather, I begin with the Scriptures about which Karl Barth has acutely said,

> It is not the right thoughts about God which form the content of the Bible but the right divine thoughts about [humankind]. The Bible tells us not how we should talk to God but what he says to us; not how we find the way to him but how he has sought and found the way to us; not the right relation in which we must place ourselves to him, but the covenant which he has made with all who are Abraham's spiritual children and which he has sealed once and for all in Jesus Christ.[5]

The creeds I have come to understand in their historical context as profound statements of faith addressed to specific or concrete situations that the church has faced across the span of time. In most instances, the creeds represent the church's reply to what it considered to be heretical teachings in its midst; (my professor of historical theology was fond of saying that heretics were those in the church who were brilliantly wrong while schismatics were obstinately wrong). It means, however, that the creeds, unless one wishes to do so, do not

4. Quoted in Richard R. Niebuhr, *Resurrection and Historical Reason* (New York: Scribner, 1957), pp. 55-56.

5. Karl Barth, *The Word of God and the Word of Man* (New York: Harper and Brothers, 1957), p. 43.

have to be taken as timeless pronouncements of Christian truth. The same professor listed two-and-a-half pages of "historic Christian creeds" and the list does not include twentieth-century formulations such as the Barmen Declaration issued by the Protestant churches in Germany against Nazi ideology in 1934, the dogma of the bodily assumption of the Virgin Mary promulgated in 1950, or the various doctrinal statements of the Second Vatican Council of 1962-65.[6] The mere mention of the latter three statements is sufficient to underscore the observation that Christians can be and are, in fact, quite selective in what they choose to accept as authoritative proclamations of Christian belief. The history of the various branches and divisions of the Christian church, in one measure, is the history of who accepts which creeds.

It also means that the task of addressing the truths of the Christian faith to specific, concrete situations the church confronts is one which must be done in every age, both now and in the future. A small band of Christians in Germany recognized that the rise of Adolf Hitler and the politics of National Socialism presented the German church with what it termed a *status confessionis* — a confessional circumstance or situation in which the church was obligated to restate what its faith meant and required in light of the Nazi assault on German society. It is a matter of deep and lasting regret that the confession issued by that band of Christians — known as the Barmen Declaration — did not respond to the two monstrous evils of the time, anti-Semitism and racism, but it was, as Paul Lehmann has written,

> the church stating and doing what it means to belong to the church of Jesus Christ in the world, on the critical boundary on which the presence and purposes of the church in and for the world and the cross-purposes of the world not only co-exist but intersect.[7]

It is a matter of continuing regret that these same twin heresies — anti-Semitism and racism — plague the world in our time but have not occasioned a *status confessionis* on the part of the churches in our era and our society. To many, this assertion will seem odd, if not out of place; are not the American churches constantly decrying racism and anti-Semitism, preaching against intolerance, and offering programs to encourage brotherhood and interfaith understanding? Yes, the churches are doing these things, but, simultaneously, there are the modern heresies — the so-called Christian Identity

6. See Jaroslav Pelikan, *The Melody of Theology* (Cambridge, Mass.: Harvard University Press, 1988), pp. 46-48.

7. Cited in Hubert G. Locke, *The Barmen Confession: Papers from the Seattle Assembly* (Lewiston, Maine: Edwin Mellen Press, 1986), p. 22.

churches, for example, which spew a concoction of biblical gibberish and racial hatred, ostensibly as expressions of Christian belief. The American churches have not seen fit to denounce those who proclaim these untruths as heretics; that is the purpose of a confession — to draw a theological line in the sand between Christian truth and falsehood.

Finally, in the same manner that I have come to view the Scriptures and the creeds of the church, I have likewise come to appreciate the richly variegated spiritual experience that is to be found in the forms and rites of worship all across the world. The music that has been composed for worship and the paintings and sculptures that adorn many churches and cathedrals are the crowning glory of the Western tradition in the arts, and they inspire me to look up and outside of myself in ways that nothing else can. Worship is always, for me, a gently powerful reminder of the ultimate wisdom of the Book of Proverbs: "trust in the Lord . . . and lean not unto thine own understanding" (3:5).

I have always found myself caught up in the deepest moments of faith and reverence when I am in a service of worship. Reading theology is an intellectual challenge but singing the great hymns of the faith or listening to the melodic chants of a choir or the magnificent strains of the organ — the very majesty and rhythm of a liturgical service or the reverent humbleness felt in the presence of a small congregation of believers — brings a sense of confidence and certainty that no amount of reasoning and reflection can muster. Dietrich Bonhoeffer, to whom we are indebted for so many powerful insights about Christian discipleship, is surely right when he says,

> Faith alone is certainty. Everything but faith is subject to doubt. Jesus Christ alone is the certainty of faith.[8]

8. Dietrich Bonhoeffer, *Ethics*, trans. Neville Horton Smith (New York: Macmillan paperback edition, 1965), p. 21.

Chapter 4

Doubt, Uncertainty, and the Death of the Six Million

Anyone who examines the Holocaust and who has even the slightest inclination to think theologically cannot help but ask: where was God while six million Jews were being slaughtered in eastern Europe between 1939 and 1945? Was God totally indifferent to what transpired in the concentration camps and killing centers of the German Third Reich? The Jews believe and Christians are taught that the Jews are God's chosen people; did God somehow decide to unchoose the Jews? Time and again the Hebrew Scriptures proclaim that God established a covenant — a formal, binding agreement — with the Jewish people, first with their patriarch Abraham and then with the entire people at Mount Sinai. What possible meaning could that or, for that matter, any covenant made with God have in the aftermath of such wanton devastation?

The murder of six million people, under any circumstances, would be horrifying enough, but these were more than six million humans. They were part of a people revered for their seemingly unique place in the history of humankind. Even their detractors take note of their endurance down through the ages; "the Jews live on," observes the historian Arnold Toynbee, " — the same peculiar people — , today, long ages after the Phoenicians and Philistines have lost their identity."[1]

Six million Jews did not die in an act of war. These were not civilians haplessly caught in the clash between opposing armies or killed in bombing raids

1. Arnold J. Toynbee, *A Study of History*, vol. 1 (London: Oxford University Press, 1946), p. 94.

This chapter is a revision of the Disciples Seminary Foundation Lecture given at the Pacific School of Religion in January 2001.

during a military conflict. That would make their deaths no less tragic but, in an age when the technology of warfare can discreetly conceal mass murder, somehow more explicable. Nor were these six million annihilated in some outburst of tribal ferocity in a remote jungle of Asia or South America. That would make their destruction more palatable to minds accustomed to think of barbarity as a distinctively primitive trait. Instead, their murder was the result of a deliberate decision made by the government of a Western power that set out to rid all the lands it conquered of the presence of the Jewish people. Nothing like this — a calculated campaign targeting a specific people for physical eradication in their entirety — had ever occurred in the history of the human species. How is it possible that it happened in a world that, according to both Jewish and Christian teaching, is under the watchful eye of its benevolent Creator who, again according to both Jewish and Christian belief, accorded the Jews a special place in God's divine economy?

For most of the three decades that I have spent in reading documents, thinking, and writing about the Holocaust, I have not tended to give much attention to the question of where God was or was not while the calamity occurred. Others have written with passion and poignancy on this troublesome problem — none more so than Richard Rubenstein, whose book, *After Auschwitz,* shattered a welter of traditional images and assumptions about the Divine. My response to these questions, for many years, was shaped by an encounter between Elie Wiesel and a brash young rabbi at the very first conference on the Holocaust and the churches, which Franklin Littell chaired and I hosted at Wayne State University in 1970. "After Auschwitz," said the young rabbi angrily, "how is it possible to believe in God?" "That," replied Wiesel calmly, "is not the question. After Auschwitz, the question is how can one believe in man?" For me, Wiesel's answer has always been the starting place for queries about the Holocaust, and it is, for the most part, the point to which I have returned at the end. After looking at the era of the German Third Reich and the ghastly events that occurred during its brief, twelve-year reign, I have been left with a profound disquiet about the human species. It has heightened my suspicion that Calvin got it right: man is born in sin and prone to evil.

Focusing on the human propensity for iniquitous behavior, however, does not permit one to escape nagging questions about God. One might assume that such questions would be especially troublesome for one who is Jewish. I have come to believe they are no less so for Christians; in fact, it is the particular claims of Christian theology that make questions about God so disturbing and the assurances of conventional Christian thought so disquieting, when both are considered in light of the massacre of the Jewish people.

Consider, for example, the liberal vision of Christianity that, as Daniel

Day Williams puts it, "sees God working in human history for a progressive achievement of a higher order of life for mankind." The culmination of God's work, Williams writes, "will be the establishment of a universal brotherhood of justice and love. . . . In the liberal perspective, we understand the meaning of our human existence when we see our place in this mighty drama of God's creative achievement."[2] But how does one account for the gruesome interruption in God's efforts that is the slaughter of millions of his covenanted people? Either we have to assert that the six million had no place in the divine drama or else that their place was the very antithesis of that which God's work was designed to achieve. Neither assertion is consistent with the liberal Christian spirit — much less with its ethic!

The conservative or evangelical Christian position is equally problematic. In the evangelical mind, God works by "supernatural intervention" in the world, the supreme moment of which is the miraculous birth of Jesus whom God sent as an atoning sacrifice for the sins of mankind. But if God intervenes in the events of history — to deliver the children of Israel from Egyptian bondage, to resurrect Jesus from death at the hands of the Romans — why did God not intervene to save the six million? The conservatives will point out, of course, that God does not always choose to intervene in the affairs and sufferings of humankind; they will point to the plight of Job who suffered as an innocent or of the Israelites whose bad fortunes under the Assyrians and the Babylonians God did nothing to prevent. This, however, only exacerbates the problem. It leaves us either with a God whose choices appear capricious and without explanation or with One whose purpose is so obscure as to be diabolical.

For evangelical Christianity, which seems to be ready with more answers than its liberal alternative, the ultimate response is to point to the crucifixion and to observe that God is no stranger not only to suffering but even to the death of the innocent. God, according to evangelical belief, was willing to endure the death of his only son because of the wickedness of the human heart. But according to evangelical dogma, the death of Jesus had a redemptive purpose; what earthly purpose, we are then led to ask, did the deaths of six million children, women, and old men serve? And assuming that their deaths were not redemptive (which the evangelical position could hardly allow) then what other possible reason might be put forth for this calamity?

Both liberal and evangelical Christianity have in common the conviction that history is the arena of God's activity — that God as well as God's purpose

2. Daniel D. Williams, *God's Grace and Man's Hope* (New York: Harper and Brothers, 1949), p. 22.

is somehow disclosed in the events that transpire in earthly time and space. For both liberal and evangelical Christians, God is intent on redeeming the world from its evil, either by using the righteous to challenge and change the structures of oppression and injustice, as liberals would hold, or by changing the hearts of sinners, as evangelicals believe. In the context of the Exodus story, for example, liberals see God as empowering the children of Israel so that they overcome the oppression of slavery. For evangelicals, God changes the heart of the Egyptian pharaoh so that Pharaoh frees his Jewish slaves.

In both cases, the action of God is seen post facto. If the problem of knowing God is that of discernment, as Daniel Day Williams postulates, then understanding God's hand in human affairs is seen in both liberal and evangelical Christian thought as a matter of reflection on events that have already transpired. Both positions would assert that we mortals cannot anticipate or predict what God will do but, in the aftermath of human events and through the eyes of faith, we are able to discern a divine purpose. But the question persists: if this is so, what possible divine purpose was achieved by the wanton annihilation of six million people?

The theological concept of a God who acts in history is the ultimate problematic for those who are preoccupied with the Holocaust and who yearn for a way of viewing that disaster that is not hopelessly at odds with two millennia of Christian thought. Those who seek to maintain the God-of-history view of the world are obliged to find a way of doing so that does not do violence to the reality and memory of six million slaughtered people.

It is possible, as some do, to dismiss all these quandaries with the judgment that — horrible though it may have been — God was punishing the Jews, either for their refusal to accept Jesus as the Messiah (as some "Christians" believe) or for some past transgression of God's Law (as more than one Jewish rabbi has proclaimed). This, tragically, is a logical consequence of the perspective that sees history as a divine-human drama and views key events in history as episodes in what the German theologians call *Heilsgeschichte,* or holy history.

The repulsiveness of this position as a religious answer to the monstrous tragedy of the twentieth century speaks for itself. As a theme in Jewish thought, it has been rejected decisively by Rubenstein, who states,

> Traditional Jewish theology maintains that God is the ultimate, omnipotent actor in the historical drama. It has interpreted every major catastrophe in Jewish history as God's punishment of a sinful Israel. I fail to see how this position can be maintained without regarding Hitler and the SS as instruments of God's will. The agony of European

> Jewry cannot be likened to the testing of Job. To see any purpose in the death camps, the traditional believer is forced to regard the most demonic, inhuman explosion in all history as a meaningful expression of God's purposes. The idea is simply too obscene for me to accept.[3]

It must, it seems to me, be rejected with equal decisiveness in Christian thought as well.

In the search, then, for answers or an answer to the question — Where was God when, during the Second World War, six million Jews went to their deaths to satisfy the perverse racial policy of the Nazi government? — we are confronted both by a concrete historical fact and by the Ultimate Abstraction. Regarding the first instance, Daniel Day Williams reminds us that

> all our human knowing comes through particular experiences. We always experience in particular ways, here and now. In short, our knowledge of anything is historical. It is derived from concrete happenings through which the real order of things is disclosed to us.[4]

It is in the light of this concrete happening that we call the Holocaust that we wrestle with the second problem: the difficulty of trying to grasp the presence — or the absence — of that which, in Williams's words, "underlies the structure of the world." If Barth is right, of course, we cannot grasp God — whether as Ultimate Reality or as Ground of Being or in any other terms. We may search for God but we can only be grasped by God. God is known — God's purpose and will is discerned — only as God discloses to us. But this only leads us once again to ask, what then was God disclosing in the Holocaust? No matter whether we try to find meaning in the events of history or whether God is seeking to grasp us in the concrete events of human experience, the question persists: what divine will or purpose can be discerned in what was a massive and brutal act of genocide?

However we imagine God to be — Ultimate Reality, Ground of Being, Ruler of the Universe, First Principle — when we look at the terrible event that scarred the human landscape in the midst of World War II, the virtual destruction of European Jewry, we are forced to rethink nearly all that we have been taught regarding the Source of all existence. We can no longer think about God without trying to make sense of the death of the six million; and we cannot think about the annihilation of the Jews of Europe without asking about God and God's will and purpose in the world.

3. Richard Rubenstein, *After Auschwitz* (Indianapolis: Bobbs-Merrill, 1966), p. 153.
4. Williams, *God's Grace*, p. 49.

I AM OBVIOUSLY NOT the first to be troubled by questions of the divine and the demonic or, in this instance, to be unsettled by the reality of the Holocaust and the seeming remoteness of God. Almost instinctively, in fact, I find myself turning to the theological literature for guidance on these perplexing issues. In the preface to his multi-volume *Systematic Theology,* Paul Tillich expressed the hope that his students, to whom he dedicated his monumental work, would find it "a help in answering the questions they are asked by people inside and outside their churches." He suggests, by implication, that helping to answer questions ought to be the aim of every theological system.

When it comes to the death of the six million, the theological literature is of three distinct types. In the first category is the bulk of Christian theological reflection since 1945, which, for all practical purposes, proceeds as though the Holocaust never occurred or, in some cases, simply accepts the actions of the Third Reich (and, in so doing, "ignores" the horror of the Holocaust). A much smaller corpus becomes enmeshed in such guilt over the failure of the Christian community to mount any significant opposition to the annihilation of European Jewry that it is unable to offer any clear or concrete guidance on questions of faith and doubt; it speaks only of endless remorse. Finally, there is a collection of writings — smaller still but immensely provocative — that confronts directly the questions of guilt, faith, and doubt that the Holocaust engenders; the answers it suggests are illuminating but immensely disturbing to one who wishes to cling to the traditional tenets of the Christian faith.

In the first category is Bernhard Anderson's *Rediscovering the Bible.* I can still remember the excitement, over forty years ago and in my first year in seminary, with which I read that work. Forty years later, I read it sorrowfully as a classic example of Christian theology in the postwar era which was untouched by the Holocaust. The subtitle of Anderson's work, *The Unfolding Drama of God's Dealing with Men,* states the book's thesis: "history," as seen by Anderson in the accounts told in the Scriptures, "is the theater in which God, the Aggressor, establishes and secures a beachhead in his struggle against the opposing force of man's sin."[5]

The arena of history, for Anderson, constitutes not only the unique series of events in which God is revealed or exposed, such as the Exodus and the incarnation. "There is a sense," Anderson writes, "in which God acts in *all* human history, even when men are unaware of his presence and his purpose. . . ."[6] "The Christian will claim that the Christian interpretation of history [i.e., that Christ 'gives the clue to the meaning of all history'] makes

5. Bernhard Anderson, *Rediscovering the Bible* (New York: Association Press, 1951), p. 24.
6. Anderson, *Rediscovering the Bible,* p. 25. Emphasis in original.

sense, and that it most adequately deals with all dimensions of human experience."[7] That this powerful assertion could be penned barely a half-dozen years after the death camps were overrun by Allied armies only gives it added poignancy. If it advanced claims only for a set of events unique to the Christian experience, it might be plausible, but this pronouncement purports to offer the "clue to the meaning of all history." Its silence, then, about one of the most shattering events of the twentieth century — or perhaps the most shattering — is deafening.

A far more jaded case is to be found in the writings of several German theologians who were at the pinnacle of their careers during the era of the German Third Reich. Emanuel Hirsch, renowned as a major figure in twentieth-century German theology, was an important interpreter of Luther. Hirsch considered Luther's emphasis on the idea of God as the working reality behind the world to be one of the central motifs in Luther's writing. It was also central to Hirsch's theology and his politics. "Human history," he wrote, "can . . . only be understood by those who see its metaphysical core and its religious connection. Human history and notions about God belong necessarily together."[8]

Hirsch came, however, to develop what Robert Ericksen terms a "political ethic and historical-theological philosophy which welcomed and then supported the National Socialist recipe for Germany."[9] According to John Dillenberger, Hirsch came to believe that there was a close connection between "Christianity, defined in Reformation terms," and the sufferings and promises of the German nation. He wrote about the hiddenness of God in the sufferings of Germany both during and since the First World War. Hirsch felt that if the nation of Germany was defeated, Christianity in Reformation terms would also be destroyed. In short, by "shifting the emphasis slightly he was able to insist upon a close connection between the German people and God's working in the world."[10] Such convictions enabled Emanuel Hirsch to proclaim, after Hitler's appointment as Reichschancellor, that

> All of us who stand in the present moment of our Volk experience it as a sunrise of divine goodness after endless dark years of wrath and misery. We experience it with a shiver of responsibility that our Volk not squander this moment, that it take this given opportunity to begin

7. Anderson, *Rediscovering the Bible*, p. 38.

8. Quoted in Robert P. Ericksen, *Theologians under Hitler: Gerhard Kittel, Paul Althaus, and Emanuel Hirsch* (New Haven: Yale University Press, 1985), p. 129.

9. Ericksen, *Theologians*, p. 123.

10. John Dillenberger, *God Hidden and Revealed* (Philadelphia: Muhlenberg, 1953), p. 48, n. 32.

> anew and bring it about in the correct way. . . . Now new hope has been given to us. And should our hearts not burn with enthusiasm that the Protestant church now say yes to this moment, that it seize the opportunity to cooperate with redeveloping the order and style of the German Volk?[11]

By 1939, Hirsch had published a series of lectures on *The Essence of Christianity* in which he stated,

> We set our entire power of life and spirit on this, to bring our Volk and Reich into a healthy, life-protecting order, and to create for them a durable and honorable existence in the circle of the white ruling peoples, to which God has entrusted the responsibility for the history of humanity.[12]

Throughout his writings, Hirsch consistently advanced the notion that "God works in history, intersects human life, and can be recognized by man through a proper appreciation of history and a properly sensitive conscience." As Ericksen concludes, this made it possible for Hirsch "to recognize the hand of God acting in the history of the German people."[13]

Similar sentiments were expressed by Gerhard Kittel, the well-known professor of New Testament theology at Tübingen who could claim that "To come to the God of their fathers has always meant for the Jews to come to the God of history. But the history of God with the Jewish Volk has meant for two thousand years: alien status among the people of the world."[14] On the strength of this assertion, Kittel argued that there were four possible answers or solutions to what the political rhetoric of the period revealed in terming the *Judenfrage*, or "the Jewish question": extermination, which he rejects for reasons not of morality but of expediency (i.e., "it has not worked before and it will not work now");[15] Zionism, which Kittel rejects as impractical; assimilation, which would lead to race-mixing and moral decadence; and finally, giving to the Jews a guest-status. It is this fourth "solution" that Kittel advocated, and by it he meant separating the Jews from the peoples among whom they lived, depriving them of their German citizenship and imposing other hardships on them.

11. Quoted in Ericksen, *Theologians*, pp. 146-47.
12. Quoted in Ericksen, *Theologians*, p. 165.
13. Ericksen, *Theologians*, p. 145.
14. Quoted in Ericksen, *Theologians*, p. 58.
15. Ericksen, *Theologians*, p. 55.

Thus, in the minds of several of Germany's principal twentieth-century theologians, the idea of a God who works in history was not incompatible with the effort to cleanse their society of what they considered to be an alien and religiously decadent people. And what Kittel thought to be inexpedient — the first of his four "solutions" to the Jewish question — became for the Nazis their *Endlösung* or final solution to the "Jewish problem."

In sharp contrast to those who continue to do theology as if the Holocaust never occurred or who accept or even advocate the principles of the German Third Reich, we also find a genre of writings that is overwhelmed by a sense of Christian guilt and failure in the wake of the Holocaust. Here, we discover such problematic assertions as

> Today's openness of dialogue between Jews and Christians owes much to the Holocaust theologians of both religious traditions. The constant interchange between them . . . challenges the rest of us to face facts fearlessly. Like them . . . we can examine together the inflammatory question of how Christian doctrine and the preaching of the Gospel led inevitably to the fires of Auschwitz.[16]

At one level, this represents the honest attempt on the part of the Christian community to acknowledge a share of responsibility for and complicity in the calamity that swept across European Jewry. Caught up, however, in remorse over the lamentable Christian inaction, we find here an example of the tendency to make a claim that does not bear up under scrutiny. Even Jewish scholars repudiate the idea that the Holocaust was a direct or inevitable consequence of Christian teaching.

Assertions such as these also have been accompanied by efforts to find parallels between the God of Israel who shares in the suffering of his people and the God who suffers in Jesus Christ. One expression of this effort is that of Clemens Thoma, who writes,

> The glow of the Auschwitz crematorium is the beacon that lights, that guides all my thoughts. Oh, my Jewish brothers, and you as well my Christian brothers, do you not think that it mingles with another glow, that of the Cross?[17]

16. Katherine T. Hargrove, "Some Christian Views of the Holocaust," in *The Future of Jewish-Christian Relations,* ed. N. Thompson and B. Cole (Schenectady, N.Y.: Character Research Press, 1982), p. 83.

17. Clemens Thoma, *A Christian Theology of Judaism* (New York: Paulist, 1980), p. 152.

It is difficult to discern here anything more than an attempt to baptize the Holocaust and make it one more drama in the Christian saga of salvation history.

We are left, finally, to grapple with the provocative observations of a handful of Christian thinkers for whom the Holocaust is a watershed in both Judaism and Christianity. Franklin Littell, in a direct challenge to traditional Christian symbols and doctrine, speaks of "the crucifixion and resurrection of the Jewish people [as] the most important event for Christian history in centuries."[18] Alice and Roy Eckhardt have called for a radical reexamination and revision of traditional Christian teaching about both God and Jesus in the light of the Jewish massacre.[19] Paul van Buren writes,

> Surely at least our expressions of assurance that God is in control and exercises authority over the world need to be restrained and severely qualified. If God is Israel's God, then we must admit that we do not know how God stands in relation to the covenant that we had thought was binding on him as well as on Israel. That is not just Israel's problem. That is the church's problem. In the face of the uncertainty, Israel can, if it will, go right on obeying the mitzvot, the Commandments. What is the church to do when just that which it took to be its core — its faith, its trust, its confidence in God — is precisely what is now in question?[20]

For these authors, and for many others, Christians have no choice but to rework their understanding of Christian faith and teachings in light of the Holocaust. It is an imperative that I earnestly endorse.

I HAVE NO THEOLOGICAL ANSWER to the question, where was God while six million Jews were being slaughtered? But over the years that I have tried to wrestle with the reality of the virtual annihilation of European Jewry, I have become increasingly convinced that Christianity, which has erected an entire faith on the execution of one Jew, has to come to terms with (even if it cannot fully understand) the execution of six million of his kinspersons. Christianity must do so not merely because of the multiple questions surrounding the role

18. Franklin H. Littell, *The Crucifixion of the Jews* (New York: Harper and Row, 1975), p. 6.

19. See, for example, their essay "After the Holocaust: Some Christian Considerations," in *Future of Jewish-Christian Relations*, ed. Thompson and Cole.

20. In *The Death of God Movement and the Holocaust*, ed. S. R. Hayes and J. K. Roth (Westport, Conn.: Greenwood, 1999), p. 38.

of the Christian community during the Holocaust. Those questions have been examined for a half-century; the record we know to be sadly mixed, not as starkly negative as some who look only at the pronouncements of church officials or exclusively at the German churches would like to claim but neither heroic nor consistent enough to permit any sense of pride or honor on the part of Christendom.

Nor is it wholly a matter of dealing with the centuries of anti-Semitism in Christian teaching and belief. No one disputes this wretched saga; in fact, most major Christian bodies have devoted a great deal of effort to issuing apologies for this blot on the Christian record and, more substantively, to rewriting Christian catechetical materials so as to eliminate offensive phrases and references. Virtually nothing remains in this area except the New Testament itself, and while there have been proposals from some quarters that the New Testament be rewritten as well, most reasonable observers are content to recognize that there is and will always remain an arena of substantial theological disagreement between Judaism and Christianity which simply should not be allowed to descend into the racial indecencies that constitute anti-Semitism.

What is ultimately challenged by the murder of six million Jews is a triumphal Christianity that claims to be the supreme expression of the divine will, that celebrates a victory already won, a redemption already present, and that neglects the not-yet aspect of Christian eschatology. Such a Christian vision all too often presents itself as having all the answers, and easy answers at that. But this sort of Christianity requires believing in a God who breaks his word and does not keep faith with his people. As if repudiating his covenant were not enough, it depicts a God who either condemns outright the bulk of his chosen people to mass slaughter or is grossly indifferent to their fate. This is not the God of the Bible nor a God in whom anyone of sense or sensibility could trust.

As an alternative to Christian triumphalism and the spiritual hubris that accompanies it, we can begin instead and in a far more humble fashion to speak with Buber of the eclipse of God, with Luther and others of the hiddenness of God, and with Helmut Thielicke of the silence of God. The dreadful, driving need we moderns seem to have for communication and the technological ease and instantaneousness with which it can be done have perhaps also driven us to think of a talking, doing, acting God much more than is warranted. Ours is a world in which everyone is busily engaged in verbal "sharing" and feeling one another's pain. In contrast, it may be that we do best to quietly accept the message of the hymn:

> Immortal, Invisible, God only wise,
> In light inaccessible hid from our eyes . . .

Unresting, unchanging, and silent as light,
Nor wanting, nor wasting, Thou rulest in might. . . .

Buber has gently suggested that there are demonic powers in the world that can and do conceal God's presence from humankind. "What is it," he writes,

> that we mean when we speak of an eclipse of God . . . ? Through this metaphor we make the tremendous assumption that we can glance up to God with our "mind's eye," or rather being's eye, as with our bodily eye to the sun, and that something can step between our existence and his as between the earth and the sun.

But, he affirms, "the eclipse of the light of God is no extinction; even tomorrow that which has stepped in between may give way."[21] Five centuries earlier, Martin Luther had advanced his famed notion of *deus absconditus* — the hidden God who, in Ritschl's paraphrase of Luther, "is to be left to his own majesty and nature" but who also "clothes himself in his Word and offers himself to us."[22]

For me, however, the most meaningful note is that struck by Helmut Thielicke, the famed preacher of St. Michael's Church in Hamburg whose sermons during the Nazi period were so critical of the Hitler regime that he was eventually forbidden to preach. After the war, he would become professor of systematic theology and later rector of the University of Tübingen, then dean of the theological faculty and subsequently rector of the University of Hamburg. But it was during the fateful years of 1942 to 1943, before the ban was imposed, that Thielicke found himself preaching to a congregation of dispirited Germans. The war had turned against Germany and its people, who only a year or so earlier had luxuriated in the idea of *Deutschland über alles* but who, a year later, found themselves searching desperately for some explanation for the decided reversal of their national fortunes.

It was, in fact, during one of the bleakest moments in the war, the battle of Stalingrad, when it became abundantly clear that the German war machine was not invincible and when the specter of defeat first loomed large in the German imagination, that Thielicke preached a sermon on the text from Matthew 15:21-28. It is the story of Jesus' encounter with the woman from Canaan who beseeches Jesus to heal her daughter; according to the text, Jesus "answered her not a word." Thielicke proclaims,

21. In Will Herberg, *The Writings of Martin Buber* (New York: Meridian, 1956), pp. 111, 113.
22. Quoted in Dillenberger, *God Hidden*, p. 3.

> The silence of God is the greatest test of our faith. We all know this. . . . Is not God silent about Stalingrad? What do we hear above and under its ruins? Do we not hear the roar of artillery, the tumult of the world and the cries of the dying? But where is the voice of God? . . . There is neither voice nor answer.

Thielicke then recounts the story of John the Baptist, who sends two of his disciples to Jesus to ask, "Are you the one who is to come or should we look for another?" Thielicke asks,

> In despairing complaint [John] rises against this destiny of the silence of Jesus. "How long do you keep us in suspense? Tell us freely whether you are the Christ? Call down from heaven that you are. . . . Why do you allow this vacillation between faith and doubt? Why do you not make things clear, God?"[23]

I find myself wrestling with Thielicke's answer to these questions he so agonizingly raises: that "the cross was God's greatest silence" and that "even when he was silent, God suffered with us." I am drawn more and more to the truth of his observation: "How many meaningless blows of fate there seem to be! — life, suffering, injustice, death, massacres, destruction; and all under a silent heaven which apparently has nothing to say."[24] In the shadow of the Shoah, it seems to me that that has come to at least approach the cross as God's greatest silence. I doubt that I will ever come to an understanding of that wretched moment in human history. I know that I can only continue to read, to ponder . . . and to pray!

23. Helmut Thielicke, *The Silence of God* (Grand Rapids: Eerdmans, 1962), pp. 12-13.
24. Thielicke, *Silence of God,* p. 14.

Chapter 5

Uncertainty and the Enigma of Race

A few years ago I was in Cape Town, South Africa, for eight days — the guest of the Cape Town Holocaust Centre whose first anniversary I was to help commemorate by giving a public lecture. I had been to Cape Town once before and remembered it as one of the world's loveliest cities, wrapped around a majestic mountain faced with commanding outcroppings of rock appropriately named Devil's Peak, Lion's Head, and the Twelve Apostles. Cape Town is also wrapped in and warped by its recent past, which it shares with the whole of the Republic of South Africa. That past is immediately visible as soon as one leaves the airport; the main highway into the city passes a seemingly endless stretch of shacks erected — one dare not say built for that would suggest design and a sturdiness that is stunningly absent in what one sees — to house the millions of black South Africans who have streamed into the city from the so-called homelands, seeking work and the possibility of participating in what everyone heralds as "the new South Africa."

I had alerted my hosts in advance that I wished to make a trip to the townships that the sea of shacks surrounds. The townships were built beginning in the 1920s to segregate and house the non-white populace away from Cape Town whites. It is the townships that are now engulfed by mile upon mile of hovels or "informal settlements," as the collection of shacks are euphemistically called by the locals. My hosts had planned well: On a Saturday I was taken by the education director of the Holocaust Centre, the wife of a Cape Town physician, who had arranged for me to be escorted by a resident of one of the townships; she, in turn, had invited another resident — one of the political activists in the African National Congress who was incarcerated on Robben Island with Nelson Mandela — to accompany us. I saw the townships not as they are seen by the continuous parade of tourists who are driven through wide-eyed and disbelieving in air-conditioned buses but through the eyes of those who live in and experience them as home and as an everyday reality.

To grasp the significance of the townships, one must understand that they are a creation of the diabolical system that, for over a century, dictated racial separateness in South Africa. The townships precede the era of apartheid; the oldest of the Cape Town townships was constructed in 1926, several decades before the African Nationalist Party came to power in 1948 and proceeded to encase in law the structures and strictures of a rigidly segregated society. The townships were a forerunner of the apartheid system. They were designed as concentration camps; one must see them and how they are laid out to fully appreciate this blunt fact. They lie on either side of the main thoroughfare into the city. The one built in 1926 — Langa — was constructed on a garbage dump and is accessible by one major road leading from the expressway into the township center. The townships were designed with all the subtle features of incarceration centers; at the first sign of trouble, they could be sealed off, contained, and controlled with a minimum of armed effort. Internally, the townships are much like any poor, rural community one would find in the American South — a mixture of tiny, older houses in the township centers surrounded by some newer, attractive two- and three-bedroom homes that black professionals were allowed to build before the apartheid regime collapsed.

Langa township also contains the infamous hostels — two-story, cement-block barracks built by the apartheid government to house men from the homelands (hundreds of miles away) who were given passes that permitted them to work in the cities. The men were not permitted to bring their wives or children, to whom they had to return home on weekends or holidays in order to visit. The hostels consist of units with a small room containing two concrete, park table–like structures that serve as an eating, washing, and sitting area, and a closet-sized room with a hot plate that is the kitchen. Surrounding this common area are three to four sleeping rooms, each large enough to accommodate three bunks. In the apartheid era, each sleeping room housed three men; when the apartheid system collapsed, wives came to join their husbands so that each room now accommodates three couples whose privacy is provided by hanging sheets or a blanket between the bunks!

The hostels were constructed near the center of the townships so anyone driving along the highway would not see them. One would not know they were there unless, of course, one was a township resident. Now from the highway one sees neither the hostels nor the township homes; both are bordered by the shanties built on the ribbon of land between the township boundary and the highway. The shanties are the size of a small bedroom in an American home, but some house entire families. Each shanty contains a bed, a table, and a cupboard for dishes and cooking utensils. There is no electricity and no running water; one sees an almost constant procession of informal settlement dwellers carrying, in large plastic containers, water fetched from a public spigot in the township. Cooking is done outdoors over wood fires; the toilets are outhouses perched precariously on the banks of a long gully that meanders through the center of the settlement.

Unlike the United States where black and impoverished residents live in the inner sections of the major cities, in Cape Town the white populace lives in the central sectors of the city. The townships were erected for black inhabitants on the city's fringes. Consequently, today, rather than a black core surrounded by a white ring, as would be the case in most U.S. metropolitan areas, Cape Town is a white, central-city populace ringed by a black circle of townships and informal settlements that is constantly being enlarged by the new black migrants to the city.

The townships and the informal settlements are just one of the tragic legacies of an ideology of racial superiority that infested South Africa for most of the past century. That ideology produced one of the most despicable societies on human record. Its collapse, in 1992, brought down a government that — in addition to a horrid indifference to the housing conditions of black South Africans — spent eight times as much on the education of a white child as on that of a black child and virtually nothing on health care for blacks. As late as 1986, the government was spending $307 per capita for the education of a white child and $74 per capita on black students. A new government, in place only since 1994, must try to cope with this legacy of impoverishment and neglect while trying to deal with the scourge of AIDS that threatens to wipe out vast segments of the South African populace.

MIDWAY THROUGH MY Cape Town visit I read an article in one of the local papers entitled "Australia's Enduring Disgrace." Written by an Australian who is apparently living in South Africa, the article describes the plight of the Aborigine populace on the Australian continent where, according to one physician, "the Aboriginal people suffer from diseases like rheumatic fever [that disappeared from] the Edinburgh slums in the past century. Here, it is the highest ever reported in the world. Diabetes . . . affects up to a quarter of the adult Aboriginal population."

Australia, according to the article, has the distinction of being the only developed country on a World Health Organization "shame list" of countries where children are still blinded by trachoma — a disease that is entirely preventable and that is spread in conditions of poverty. A spot check of Aboriginal children showed, in some areas, a third to a half infected by the disease. Australia also has the highest death rate in the world among its Aboriginal populace; the death rate among Aboriginal women is six times that of their white Australian counterparts.

A professor at Macquarie University in Sydney, Colin Tatz is a South African political refugee who finds in Australia a reflection of his own nation and its past:

> People say to me, surely, South Africa was an example of dreadful, maniacal, premeditated racism where Australia was really a case of innocent ignorance. The truth is there is a tremendous similarity, both in ideology and notions of scientific racial theories: for example, the fuller the [Aboriginal] blood, the more primitive; the lighter the skin colour, the more salvagable. The reserves, the exploitative labour, the sexual exploitation of women, the separate health systems, the separate education, the [now-abolished] ban on inter-racial marriage — all are the same.

What is striking is how these same features of racism are to be found in every society in which this social disease of modernity has appeared. It is as though people who are white find it impossible to live alongside people who are not without engaging in the most outrageous forms of exploitation. Something seems to persuade whites that they are innately superior and thereby entitled to oppress those who do not look like themselves. The patterns of oppression then all become the same: whites see non-whites as a cheap or, in cases of slavery, a free source of labor. This, in turn, requires that the non-whites are not permitted to be educated lest they learn to become dissatisfied with their circumstances. Their health and its care become matters of indifference since their numbers are great and they can be easily replaced. And, having been assigned an inferior status in the society, all sorts of fears against mixing with them emerge and are enacted into law — including the ultimate taboo of intermarriage.

Societies do not remain static. Wherever there are conditions of human oppression, there are countervailing pressures toward human freedom and equality. Over time slavery and segregated societies give way before forces of liberation and the quest for human dignity. When this occurs, white societies characteristically turn to the law and its institutions to preserve the social inequality they have devised. The result is a massive imprisonment of the non-white populace, greatly out of proportion to their numbers in the society. Whites announce that this is because non-whites commit greater proportions of crime, conveniently ignoring the fact that, at least in the United States, huge numbers of young black males are locked up essentially for committing crimes against themselves — for drug addiction and the collateral offenses that accompany this slow form of suicide.

This is the reality I confront when I return home to a nation that has gone through the other institutional phases of racial oppression — slavery and segregation — and, now that the American economy no longer has need for the huge supply of unskilled labor that the agricultural and industrial eras required, has turned to incarceration as the answer to its perennial problem of race. By imprisoning young black males — fully one-quarter of those between the ages of eighteen and twenty-nine are either in jail or in prison — the United States has moved from treating its black populace as exploitable (as they were during slavery) to replaceable (as they were during the industrial age) to expendable (as is now the case in the digital era).

When I arrived in Cape Town, I found in my hotel room a gift graciously left by my hosts to welcome me to the city. It was a beautiful volume entitled *This Is Cape Town,* which, in pictures and text, tells the story of this magnificent city. Page after page of photographs depict the exquisite sights of the metropolis, but there are no pictures of the townships or the informal settlements.

The book serves as a pictorial metaphor of the problem of race in the modern world. Like the book, whites may simply choose to ignore the realities that constitute life as it is lived by a majority of the world's populace. Not all whites do so — my Cape Town hosts and a number of their friends were deeply engaged in the struggle for social justice in their nation, as have been many in the United States and, I'm sure, in Australia as well. But they are a minority. The majority of the white populace — not only in Cape Town but throughout the Western world — lives not only in ignorance about the life-struggles of non-whites but also in benign indifference to this latter reality. Historically, whites have behaved as though they have a natural entitlement to dominance and privilege in the world's societies. They continue to do so in spite of the fact that there are signs everywhere pointing to the horrid, societal mess this sentiment has created in the world.

I have become increasingly convinced over the years — widespread opinion to the contrary not withstanding — that this behavior of whites does not stem from outright arrogance or bigotry. That such bigotry exists among whites is not to be doubted, but it does so among a recalcitrant minority, much as those working for racial equality make up a minority on the opposite side. The behavior of most white people is simply the result of their not having to think about race and, accordingly, of being able to assume that the position they enjoy in life is the natural order of things. Nothing they encounter in their daily lives in Western societies challenges this assumption; everything, in fact, reinforces it.

Wherever whites look or turn, they see a world in which they are in charge of the events and occurrences that matter. To pick up the morning paper or tune in to the evening news is to be both reminded and, if one is white, reassured that the viewpoints that are important, the decisions that count, the judgments that are significant, the opinions that are determinative are those made by whites. Whether in the halls of Parliament or Congress, the board rooms of banks, the editorial offices of newspapers and television stations, or the corporate offices of the Fortune 500, those who call the shots tend both to look alike and to look very Anglo-Saxon. A glance at the fashions advertisements in magazines and on billboards, at the photos of CEOs on the business page, or at the members of the local symphony orchestra or ballet company, and one sees a depiction of who sets the standard for what is considered aesthetically desirable, economically progressive, or culturally uplifting in society. There has been — it is true — some measure of change in all of these arenas so that one finds some black faces and a few Asian and Hispanic ones in all these settings, but — the photos of Colin Powell and Condoleezza Rice in the media notwithstanding — the change has not been enough to alter the basic reality that anyone who is white can take for granted.

If white people do not have to think about race and can take their dominance in society for granted, then the opposite is true for non-whites in general and for black people in particular. It may be discounted as a matter of gross paranoia but, for people of color, the fact is that living in a white-dominated society means being constantly reminded not only that one is not white and therefore different but also that one is "disenfranchised," not entitled to the rights and privileges that whites have by mere fact of the color of their skin. It can be, in fact, such a source of paranoia that those blacks who are unable to come to terms with the constant presence of race in their lives become, in their own tragic way, racists-in-reverse who come to think of everything black as superior to everything that is white.

Much is made these days of something called "white privilege" — those benefits and opportunities that come to white persons simply because of their skin color. Of all the racial privileges that whites enjoy, however, none is greater than that of not having to think about race. In this lies the conundrum of race in the modern world. To be white is to be spared the constant reminder of one's status and place in society and of how — if one is not white — one is likely to be perceived by those who are in charge of society's daily processes: by teachers who assume intellectual inferiority, by police officers who presume some inclination toward criminality, by co-workers and bosses who think one's job is owed to affirmative action, and by politicians who find the non-white populace a perfect foil for whatever fears or anxieties seekers of public office wish to feed. Very little of this takes place overtly these days; that would be considered crude in a society that prides itself on its civic sophistication. But precisely because it takes more subtle forms and expressions, it is all the more insidious.

I suspect, in fact, if most black people in America were asked what their one great desire would be (when it comes to race relations), it would not be for an expansion of affirmative action programs or reparations for the unrecompensed labor of their slave ancestors or any other specific program or project. It would simply be to not have to think about race as a constant in their lives. Achieving this, of course, would mean reconstructing American society so that the reality of everyday life matched the rhetoric the nation proclaims about itself. In the United States it would require excising from our national life not the reality of differences in the populace but the assumptions and stereotypes that accompany those differences. It would oblige us, in brief, to build a nation in which there is genuine "liberty and justice for all."

The United States wrestles with the problem of race in its own peculiar fashion, but at the core of the problem in America is the fact that black and white Americans live not in one nation, let alone "under God," but on two entirely different planets. This is the only metaphor that accurately depicts the gulf that lies between the lives and experiences of black Americans and their white counterparts. As much as we might like to think — or wish — that this chasm has been bridged, it remains an enduring feature of the American racial landscape. It is tragically true even of integrated neighborhoods and workplaces and in spite of genuine efforts of people on both sides of the racial divide to lessen the distance between the two peoples.

The depths of this chasm can be seen in many ways and in many diverse settings. It is especially visible whenever there are public incidents such as the shooting of a black person by a police officer, a high profile crime in which the perpetrator is or is alleged to be black, or any other circumstance that invites interpretation or explanation, either by the media acting in their self-anointed role as keeper of the public conscience or by the public itself, seeking to make some sense out of a tragic or emotional event in a community.

If it is a police shooting — and these occur with such saddening frequency that they become almost routine flash points for increased tensions in black-white relations — the response on both sides of the racial divide is rather predictable. Black Americans will decry the incident — whatever its particular circumstances might be — as one more example of police racism and brutality. White Americans, however, are likely to ask why black Americans leap to racism as the explanatory cause of every volatile encounter between the police and black citizens and, if there is the least questionable circumstance in the black victim's background, assume that circumstance is sufficient warrant for the police action, fatal though the outcome often may have been.

Each group views the matter from its own set of premises and experiences. For black people, especially if they live in the inner-city neighborhoods of large, urban areas, their experiences often include residing in communities where crime is a persistent problem (as it is in nearly all economically deprived areas) and where policing is likely to be carried out with an especial aggressiveness. The corresponding likelihood is that large numbers of residents of such communities will have had negative, personal encounters with police officers — being stopped and questioned, having their vehicles searched, or being cited for some minor infraction of the law — particularly if the residents are male and if they are young. Nearly every black male in America, in fact — no matter what his status, educational background, or profession — has his own personal story of an irritating or infuriating encounter with a police officer that left an unforgettable, bad taste in his mouth about American law enforcement.

When a police shooting occurs, therefore, black people are inclined to assume the worst about the police officer involved, simply because, in city after city across the nation, encounters between the police and black citizens tend to be so uniformly negative. Black citizens will express dismay at the fact that the offense involved in a police shooting is, in nearly every instance, not one for which the offender (if arrested, tried, and convicted) would have to forfeit his life. And because the occasions are extremely rare in which a police officer is charged — let alone convicted — in the death of a black person, the suspicion is only increased that the police may conduct themselves toward black Americans with impunity.

White Americans, as a group, tend not to have unpleasant encounters with the police. At the least, white citizens do not find themselves in situations (as black citizens can) in which the color of their skin is itself a badge of suspicion. White Americans, therefore, have no experiential frame of reference within which to understand the almost innate assumptions, fears, and hostilities that drive the reactions of overwhelming numbers of black people toward the police. This same lack of an experiential frame extends into countless other day-to-day situations in which, for all practical purposes, black and white people simply live in two different worlds. As a consequence, the communication between the two groups — often filtered through media stories, letters to the editor, or angry, uninformed outbursts on radio and television talk shows that frequently are deliberately designed to exacerbate, rather than alleviate, racial tension and conflict — proceeds as though the two groups were standing on the opposite sides of a great rift, shouting audible but unintelligible accusations at one another. It is why, if measured by the degree of civil discourse between black and white Americans, race relations in the United States have not progressed substantially beyond where they were a generation ago.

SINCE A PART OF OUR national rhetoric says our nation stands "under God," it may be asked what, if anything, God has to do with this troublesome business of race, or, perhaps more importantly, what does the business of race have to do with faith in God? The latter is easier to answer than the former.

Faith in God, it seems, instills in people who are on the receiving end of racial oppression an enormous and extraordinary capacity for forgiveness. This appears as one of the astonishing features in the history of the quest for justice in the twentieth century. In South Africa, where virtually everyone predicted that the collapse of a society built on the principle of apartheid would, if it ever occurred, be accompanied by a bloodbath of unimaginable proportions, just the opposite transpired. Rather than revenge and retribution, the African people responded to their white colonizers with an insistence on truth and reconciliation! Consequently, members of the white South African Defence Force, which enforced the laws of the apartheid regime with unspeakable ruthlessness, had only to acknowledge their roles in the brutal regime and to express regret for their actions — and they were exonerated. In the United States, three decades earlier, black Americans in the South responded to a century of segregation and second-class citizenship with massive, peaceful protests and a nonviolent demand for change. They faced, in the process, outbursts of barbarism on the part of a segment of southern whites that seemed to know no bounds. In both countries, the efforts toward racial equality were led by people of faith: the Commission on Truth and Reconciliation in South Africa was chaired by the African Archbishop of Cape Town while the struggle to end segregation in the American South was led by a black Baptist preacher from Montgomery, Alabama.

Cynics will immediately note that faith in God is not the possession only of those who are recipients of racial oppression but of their oppressors as well. It does give one pause to wonder why religious faith produces saints and sinners alike. This, however, is a problem for others to sort out; I tend not to be interested in the psychopathology of religion but in religion's finer moments — in its powerful impact and influence in the lives of men and women who pursue justice and peace, rather than disharmony and conflict, in the world.

It is here that the record of black South Africans and black Americans is so remarkable. If the history of Europe for over four hundred years and until relatively recently is the chronicle of repeated conflict between peoples whose ills — real and imagined — have propelled them into an unending series of bloody clashes with one another, then the saga of black Americans and black South Africans has been one of a fierce determination to wipe out the institutions and structures of racist regimes by, in biblical terms, "overcoming evil with good." Given the propensity of contemporary white commentators to dwell on the shortcomings of black African political leaders (and the egotistical proclivities of a few of their black American counterparts), it is worth underscoring this distinctive feature of modern black history in this nation and in South Africa.

The corresponding question — What God has to do with the intractable business of race? — has always been a troublesome one for me, as it has to be for anyone who takes faith in God and the realities of racism seriously. As a first consideration, all the attributes that the Jewish and Christian Scriptures ascribe to God are made a mockery by the very presence of racism in the world. If God is Creator, it is a cruel joke to make (or to permit the evolution of, to be more scientifically accurate) a sizable portion of the world's populace with visible features that become the occasion for oppression, exploitation, and mockery by the rest of God's creation. If God is omniscient, surely he would have foreknown the unspeakable cruelty that accompanies racial differences in the world. It seems that the God who is omnipotent ruler of the universe must, in fact, be an impotent being in the face of the undiminished injustices that reign in the world in the name of racial superiority. And if God is Love, then, when it comes to race, love's opposite is a far more powerful force in human history.

It is easy to see, when contemplating the enigma of race in the modern world, how early Christians were tempted by the teachings of Manichaeism and the Gnostics. Here, at least, were religious thinkers who took the presence of evil in the world seriously. They understood that the conventional Christian answer to the problem of evil — that God gave humans free will and the power to choose between good and evil — is not a very satisfactory one; if God created humans with the capacity to choose evil, then the giver of such a "fatal gift," as a noted Indian scholar observes, becomes "the cause of pain and evil" in the world.[1] Placing the blame on humans for the racial ills of the world rightly identifies the most obvious culprits, but it does not resolve completely the problem of responsibility.

Race and racism are also, as we have seen in connection with the death of the six million, a particular problem for that perspective in Jewish and Christian thought which emphasizes a God who is active in human history. Here, one is likely to hear much about the God who raised up Moses to lead the children of Israel out of Egyptian bondage, who delivered Daniel from the den of lions and the Hebrews from a furnace of fire, and whose supreme act of redemption was sending Jesus Christ into the world to die for the sins of humanity. But the God who brought the Israelites out from under the yoke of Egyptian bondage was a God who permitted generations of their forebears to suffer as slaves; the ancestors of those who escaped Egypt must surely have wondered why God did not see fit to act in their time. And if God acts in some moments in history, why not in others? Why especially has God not acted in the untold number of occasions when the evil of racism has been on display?

I find, then, that I must abandon most of the concepts and depictions of God on which I was raised and nurtured for much of my life. They simply do not mesh with nor are they adequate for the world that I and so many people like me experience in our daily existence. They are, in fact, images of God that fit best with the experiences and societies of people who dominate rather than with those who are dominated — God as Almighty, as Ruler, as King. It tempts one to suspect that those dominating concepts of God are the creations of people who not only imagine God in their own image but who also find it useful to portray the Divine in ways that confirm the propriety of their own behavior.

I also find, however, that I have a growing unease with this monologue with myself. I fear I may be committing the mistake we humans so often make when we think about God — of trying to cram the Divine into our narrow set of concerns and issues. One part of me says that trying to do so is only natural: how can we worship a God whose being or character we cannot fathom or who is depicted in ways that clash with the realities of our own lives? But the other part reminds me that I was raised in a tradition that

1. S. Radhakrishnan, *Eastern Religions and Western Thought* (Oxford: Clarendon, 1939), p. 126.

chides those who think they can understand the ways of God; "my ways are not your ways, nor my thoughts your thoughts," says the Lord, "for as the heavens are high above the earth, so are my ways above your ways and my thoughts above your thoughts" (Isaiah 55:8-9).

There is also something deep within me that wishes to disconnect God totally from the problem of race. For all the intellectual misgivings such a disconnection poses, somehow associating the Highest that we are able to imagine with one of the lowest of the human instincts is its own form of blasphemy. It also diverts attention from the real source of the problem: those attitudes and assumptions that lead anyone to think that there are racially superior and inferior people on this planet. Such persons — and not God — are responsible for continual mayhem and misery in the world.

That leaves us with the church — ostensibly the kingdom of God on earth and the prototype of the heavenly kingdom which is to come. The church is appropriately a focus of attention regarding the question of race chiefly because it claims so much for itself. It declares itself to be the body of Christ, the visible representation and reflection of what Christianity is. It holds itself forth as the repository of Christian truths and of the values associated with the Christian life. One would hope the church might offer the solution to the problem of race; instead, it is a major part of the problem.

That problem does not stem from the much-touted observation that Sunday morning at 11 A.M. is the most segregated hour in America. If that were the problem, black Christians would bear as much of the blame as their white counterparts, for the fact that churches are segregated is as much due to black parochialism as it is to white provincialism. The problem exists on a far larger, international scale and relates primarily to the fact that Christians and their churches have never been able to successfully overcome the temptation to equate Christianity and nationalism as two sides of the same coin.

In European Christianity, where this problem is the most apparent, the church serves as the religious reflection of the state: its edifices are built by the state, its clergy are paid by the state, its hospitals, schools, and homes for the orphaned, the elderly, and the infirm all carry out functions on behalf of the state. There is, of course, nothing inherently wrong with this arrangement except that it reinforces the assumption, in many European nations, that Christianity is merely one more feature or element in what it means to be a Dane, a Serb, or a British subject. Rather than seeing themselves as Christians who are Danish, Serbian, or British, the perception flows in the other direction, and, consequently, when national identity is challenged or threatened, Christian convictions and commitments are powerless to serve as a corrective to raw nationalist instincts.

In modern-day Serbia and in Germany a half-century ago, this problem reached barbaric proportions. But it is no less a fundamental problem in postwar Germany, France, Belgium, and Scandinavia — even if its manifestations are less crude. These nations currently find themselves coping with rising tides of resentment regarding the numbers of foreign persons in their midst; one of the most frequent complaints is that the newcomers do not "integrate" themselves into the dominant culture. This grievance tends to mask a far deeper misgiving linked to the fact that the newcomers are not of the same racial stock. Christians who are taught that "God has made of one blood all the nations of the earth" (Acts 17:26) should be able to rise above these narrow, nationalist sentiments; instead the churches both reflect and perpetuate them.

In the United States, where official ties between church and state do not exist, the problem is no better and, in some respects, far worse. Many American churches are notorious for confusing Christianity with capitalism and the American way of life, while others equate the Christian faith with Southern culture or some other equally idolatrous substitute for authentic Christianity. In nearly all these religious arenas, race is considered a "problem of the [individual] heart," not an issue of collective social responsibility. This posture produces Christians who are full of compassion when confronted by an individual in need or a family in distress but who are impervious to the consequences of public policies that have disastrous consequences for racial groups. The death penalty, for example, is one such policy. The fact that it adversely affects huge numbers of black and Hispanic Americans, that it is employed most routinely in states where the fortunes of people of color have never been a matter of equitable treatment, that it is imposed most frequently when a person of color is found guilty of a capital crime against a white victim — all this is ignored or deemed irrelevant by Christian supporters of the death penalty.

The church, therefore, has yet to come to terms with the problem of race, either in America or elsewhere in the world. Until it does, race will remain the Achilles' heel of the Christian message — one of the significant points at which Christian rhetoric does not match the reality of the Christian world.

It is difficult to avoid despair about the problem of race and the possibility of its ever being resolved, but in the final analysis I am sustained by the conviction of the Psalmist. In one of the most magnificent prayers to be found in the Hebrew Scriptures, the petitioner opens with the majestic declaration:

> The Lord is my light and my salvation;
> whom shall I fear?
> The Lord is the stronghold of my life;
> of whom shall I be afraid?

But almost as if the very questions the Psalmist asks himself prompt the need to be specific about his fears, he then proceeds to recite a litany regarding the "evildoers," "adversaries," and "foes" who surround him. His despair deepens as his recitation proceeds, so that he feels forsaken even by his own parents. But then comes his affirmation of faith:

> I believe that I shall see the goodness of the Lord
> in the land of the living!
> Wait for the Lord;
> be strong, and let your heart take courage;
> yea, wait for the Lord! (Psalm 27 RSV)

The King James translation of the penultimate verse of this Psalm is even more poignant: "I had fainted unless I had believed to see the goodness of the Lord in the land of the living." Or, to rephrase, "God forgive me if I were to doubt that I shall see the goodness of the Lord in the land of the living." As one of the commentaries observes, the latter reading is the more human. It captures the pervasive uncertainty about the possibility of goodness and justice in this life that anyone feels who looks at the world and its discord. It also admits the very human temptation to doubt whether there is such a thing as "God's goodness." But, in the end, it affirms the belief in that goodness and that it will ultimately prevail.

If God is just, then this assuredly will be the ultimate answer to the unending question of race and all of its sad consequences in human history.

Chapter 6

Doubt, Faith, and the Scriptures

I take some comfort in the fact that doubt is not an act of unbelief; in fact and ironically, doubt may be a supreme act of faith and devotion. If this is too much to claim, at the least doubt is something that Scripture understands and for which the Bible has the utmost sympathy.

At first glance, this would seem not to be the case. There are repeated chastisements about and warnings against doubt throughout the Gospels and Paul's epistles. In Matthew's account, when Peter attempts to walk on the surface of the lake as Jesus had but is seized with fear and begins to sink, Jesus says to him, "why did you doubt?" or "why did you hesitate?" (14:31). Later, when they are en route to Jerusalem, Jesus tells all the disciples accompanying him, "if only you have faith and have no doubts . . . whatever you pray for in faith you will receive" (21:21-22). Mark's Gospel, which recounts this same incident, recalls Jesus saying, "Have faith in God. If anyone . . . has no inward doubts . . . then whatever you ask for in prayer, believe that you have received it and it will be yours" (11:22-24). Jesus even admonishes his followers "not to be of doubtful mind" regarding their daily necessities — what they will eat or drink — for "your Father knows you have need of these things" (Luke 12:29-30).

Paul turns this whole business of faith and doubt on end by declaring that Christians who are doubtful about eating certain foods condemn themselves because they do not act in faith; elsewhere, Paul reminds Timothy that he desires those who pray to do so "without doubting" (1 Timothy 2:8). Finally, there is the famed passage in the Epistle of James referred to earlier:

> If any of you falls short in wisdom, he should ask God for it and it will be given him, for God is a generous giver who neither refuses nor reproaches anyone. But he must ask in faith, without a doubt in his

> mind; for the doubter is like a heaving sea ruffled by the wind. A man of that kind must not expect the Lord to give him anything; he is double-minded, and can never keep a steady course. (1:5-8)

It may be, however, that these declarations are made in large part because of the persistent doubt among both Jesus' principal followers and his disciples. Matthew recounts that after Jesus' death, the eleven remaining apostles made their way to Galilee where they saw the risen Lord. Some, says Matthew, "fell prostrate before him, but some were doubtful" (28:17). The book of Acts records that several months later, when the apostles were observing the festival of Pentecost and experienced the sudden presence of God's Spirit, the crowd that gathered was bewildered because each person could understand the apostles in his own language. And the crowd, who would subsequently form the nucleus of the first congregation of Christians, "were all amazed and were in doubt" (2:12) because they did not know or understand what this extraordinary event meant.

Episodes and incidents of doubt, therefore, appear throughout Scripture. Alongside the recitations of faith are recorded the moments of uncertainty and hesitation — "some fell prostrate . . . but some were doubtful." The Bible makes no attempt whatsoever to cover up or gloss over those occasions when some persons, individually or collectively, expressed misgiving about Jesus, his message, and especially his several appearances to his followers after his execution. Each of the four Gospels, in fact, is at pains to point out the extent to which Jesus' resurrection appearances were greeted with skepticism in many quarters. Matthew's comment has already been noted. Mark records that when Mary of Magdala carried the news of his resurrection to his mourning and sorrowful followers, "they did not believe it" (16:11). Luke similarly states that when a group of women reported seeing the risen Christ, "the story appeared to [the apostles] to be nonsense, and they would not believe them" (24:10-11). But it is the Gospel of John that tells the story of the skeptic par excellence, to which we shall turn shortly.

From a modern, marketing point of view, advertising a new product with stories of the number of consumers who disbelieve its claim is a very questionable way to go about launching a new commodity. Putting the matter in these contemporary business terms risks sounding slightly blasphemous, but it is the best way, perhaps, of underscoring the fact that this new movement that would come to be called "The Way" and much later "Christianity" got its start by being ruthlessly forthright about the number of people who did not put much stock in its principal message. Here were followers of Jesus, anxious to attract other disciples who would spread the good news that the Messiah of

God had come to earth; but they did so by acknowledging that the very act that confirmed Jesus as the Christ — as God's anointed — was one that many would find incredible. At the outset of the Christian movement, therefore, the earliest disciples of Jesus made room for disbelief as well as for faith!

It is clear from the accounts noted thus far that doubt is not necessarily unbelief. Doubt is not denial; in many instances, it is bewilderment, as it was when Jesus told his disciples that one of them would betray him. One translation says the disciples looked at one another, "doubting of whom he spake" (John 13:22 KJV); an alternate translation says the disciples looked at one another "in bewilderment; whom could he be speaking of?" (NEB). Doubt, therefore, should not be lumped together with cynicism. The doubter is not the person who views every new situation with suspicion; rather, the person who doubts is often one who greets much of life with astonishment and hesitancy. It is not that the doubter finds others untrustworthy or undependable or that she is inclined to expect the worst of others. The doubter prefers to ponder and weigh life's circumstances and, in the final analysis, to take a carefully measured approach to whatever is to be confronted.

We shall see these qualities clearly in two of the three biblical characters we shall examine more closely. First, however, it is important to remind ourselves that the Bible consists not only of precepts and maxims; it is also filled with the life stories of men and women who searched for God. Some, like Noah and Abraham, were firmly convinced they had found God and were following in the footsteps of the Divine. Others, like David, were less sure; at times they walked with God, while at other times they followed their own will and ways. Still others were not always certain, either about God or about themselves. It is this final group who merit our particular attention.

Job

We begin with that tragically heroic figure in the Hebrew Scriptures who is probably one of the most admired and least understood persons in the entire Bible. He has been held forth for ages as the veritable model of patience, but only those who have never read his story could make such an immense misjudgment, for Job is a man of outraged impatience. In the book that bears his name, Job argues with his four friends, but his quarrel is really with God; one of his regrets — which he expresses continuously — is that he cannot conduct his quarrel with God face-to-face. And when we listen to his complaint, it is difficult to escape the utmost sympathy for Job's plight.

Job's story is a heartrending one, although it can be told more easily if one skips the prologue (1:6-12; 2:1-7b), which has God and Satan virtually wagering about whether Job is as righteous as he appears. Job is presented as a man who is "blameless and upright," blessed with a large family of ten children, with huge herds of camels, sheep, donkeys, and oxen, and with a great many servants. Job is, in fact, a man of some prominence in the region where he lives and, central to the story's plot, he is such a righteous person that when his children have enjoyed a holiday, Job prays on their behalf, in case they might inadvertently have said or done something that would offend God.

Quite suddenly, however, a series of calamities befall Job. His livestock and the servants attending them are set upon by raiders and killed. A tornado strikes the home of Job's eldest son where Job's children had gathered for a celebration of some sort; the house collapses and all Job's offspring are killed. "In all this," the narrative says, "Job did not sin or charge God with wrong" (1:22).

Then physical misfortune strikes Job himself. He is afflicted with a horrid rash "from the sole of his foot to the crown of his head" (2:7); his wife suggests that he simply get it over with by cursing God and suffering the death she was sure would accompany such blasphemy. But Job rebukes his wife by pointing out that if mortals receive good from God's hands, should they not also expect that there will be times when they receive evil as well? And again we are told, "in all this Job did not sin with his lips" (2:10).

But now the scene and the story shift dramatically. Three old friends of Job hear of his misfortune and come to console him. Whether it is their appearance, or the fact that Job has had time to mull over his accumulated tragedies, or the growing realization that he is the recipient of a really raw deal, we do not know. We only know that suddenly Job begins to express, in increasingly harsh and vituperative terms, his bitterness over his plight and his doubt about the God who is the cause of it all.

His friends — good, orthodox believers that they are — seek to convince Job that he himself is the reason for his own calamity. They remind Job that he has counseled and supported others in the past who were experiencing some misfortune; now, they suggest, it is Job's turn to suffer. They realize that he is understandably impatient. But "think now," one of the friends says, "who that was innocent ever perished? Or where were the upright cut off?" (4:8). For Job's friends, the answer to his lament is simple. In some way or manner, perhaps without realizing it, Job has sinned against God, and all his misfortunes are punishment for his sin.

Job, however, is not at all receptive to this argument. "If you can teach me and make me understand how I have erred," he retorts, "I will be silent"

(6:24). And anticipating that his friends will not be able to do so, Job rushes on: "I will not restrain my mouth. I will speak in the anguish of my spirit" (7:11). He then turns to God in the first of a series of outbursts and cries out: "Leave me alone. . . . Why have you made me your mark? Why have I become a burden to you? . . . Soon I will lie in my grave; you will seek me, but I will not exist" (7:16-21).

Job's friends persist in the attempt to link Job's suffering with some sinfulness on his part, perhaps a sin of which he is unaware. "If you are pure and upright," they say, "then God will rouse himself for you and reward you with a rightful habitation; God will not reject a blameless person" (8:6, 20). But this refrain clearly begins to grate on Job, who says rhetorically, "I will say to God, let me know why you contend against me. Do not condemn me . . . for you know, God, that I am not guilty" (10:2, 7). So his friends take a slightly different tack. They point out that, mere mortal that he is, Job cannot understand the mysteries of the divine mind. "Can you find out the deep things of God? Can you find out the limit of the Almighty? It is higher than heaven — what can you do? Deeper than Hell — what can you know?" (11:7-8).

Job's response turns to sarcasm, "No doubt wisdom will die with you," he says to his friends, "but I can understand things just as well as you; I am not your inferior!" (12:2-3). Rather, he continues, he is a just and blameless man, but one who has become a laughingstock to his friends; he is looked upon as a man who called upon God and whom God answered — with an endless torrent of miseries.

There follow two of the most eloquent — and contradictory — soliloquies in the entire Job saga. First Job cries, "Man that is born of a woman is of a few days, and full of trouble. He comes forth like a flower and withers; he flees like a shadow and does not continue" (14:1-2). Until recently, this lament of Job was often read as the opening words at a Christian burial service. If this chapter is read in its entirety, however, it seems like the antithesis of any belief in immortality. There is hope for a tree, Job goes on to say, that if it is cut down, it will nevertheless sprout again; "water will cause it to bud and put forth branches like a young plant" (14:9). But mortals die and are laid low; they breathe their last, and where are they, he asks?

> As waters fail in a lake and a river wastes away and dries up, so man lies down and rises not again; till the heavens are no more he will not awake or be roused out of his sleep. . . . If a man die, shall he live again? (14:11-14)

Job leaves this question unanswered!

Following this, Job's attempt at dialogue with God grows more intense — and more acerbic — until he finally cries out, "know then that God has put me in the wrong. . . . I cry out 'Violence!' but I am not answered. I call aloud but there is no justice" (19:6-7). Shortly thereafter follows the second soliloquy. As the King James renders it:

> For I know that my Redeemer liveth,
> and that he shall stand at the latter day upon the earth:
> And though after my skin worms destroy this body,
> yet . . . shall I see God:
> Whom I shall see for myself,
> and mine eyes shall behold, and not another. . . . (19:25-27)

I have omitted, in this citation, what are either three or four critical words. The King James Version reads, "And though after my skin worms destroy this body, yet *in* my flesh shall I see God." The American Standard Version says, "Then *without* my flesh shall I see God." The difference — and it is an enormous one — has to do with the translation of one small Hebrew preposition which can mean either "from within" or "from without." The commentaries wax endlessly on this textual problem, offering all sorts of linguistic, theological, and contextual reasons for the one reading or the other. In the end, it is the King James rendering that is at the core of the traditional Christian belief in the resurrection of the body, while the American Standard translation is the less offensive to the modern mind that wishes to take immortality seriously without dismissing the reality of the body's decay after death.

However this passage is to be rendered, clearly Job is not of one mind regarding the idea of immortality. If his latter soliloquy is taken, as it is in the Christian tradition, as one of the most profound and poetic expressions of a belief in immortality, then there is the earlier passage to contend with, in which Job expressed rank pessimism about the prospect of a life after death. At best, we have to deal with a man who seems torn by two distinct possibilities and who is not certain which is the truer assertion.

Job's argument with his friends and his dispute with God continue and, in the end, God answers Job in a manner that is almost as disturbing as the conversation between God and Satan at the story's outset. At the heart of the story, however, is Job's doubt. He rejects out of hand his friends' view that his troubles are the deserved consequence of his own sinfulness. He is equally disdainful of the view that the wicked will receive their just desserts. Ultimately, Job is skeptical of the idea that God is either just or compassionate, for his circumstances contradict any such claims!

We may ask how such a story, which begins with the assertion that in spite of his misfortunes Job "did not charge God with wrong" but proceeds to spend most of the remaining narrative detailing precisely such a charge, ever found its way into the canon of Holy Scripture. Given all the exhortations against doubters and doubting in the Gospels and Paul, this is a strange account to include in the Bible! It is a strange account indeed — unless its purpose is to make clear that there are things we mortals will always and necessarily confront as matters of doubt and uncertainty. God's answer to Job's complaint is, in large measure, precisely this assertion — bad things do happen to good people and there is no rational, logical, or theological answer to the problem.

In such circumstances, the Bible seeks to assure us by stories like that of Job that our doubts and misgivings are not acts of irreverence. Like our trust and confidence in those close to us — friends and family — our faith in God is also at times put to the test by situations we do not understand or cannot grasp. But as with family and friends, where we count on the depth and endurance of the relationship to sustain and overcome its momentary dislocations, so also with God, in whose ultimate faithfulness to us we trust.

Thomas

He has been popularly called "doubting Thomas," and for very good reason! Thomas was confronted with a situation that defied all known logic and common sense. Unlike Job, whose doubt concerned the justice and compassion of God, Thomas was asked to believe not in God or God's goodness but in another mortal with whom he had spent some three years as a companion. He lived through the final days of this mortal's life, saw him arrested, knew of his trial and sentence, and knew that the sentence of death had been carried out. He may, in fact, have been present when it was. But he found himself asked to believe that the man he had come to call Lord was not dead but had been somehow brought back to life. And faced with those facts he was incredulous.

Thomas is one of the curious biblical figures about whom we instinctively wish we knew more. All four Gospels make mention of him but, with the exception of John, tell us very little about him. In John's Gospel, it is Thomas who seems to have a pragmatic streak about him: when Jesus tries to warn his close companions of his imminent death by telling them that he is going to his Father's house "to prepare a place" for them — a place which, Jesus says, they know and the way to which they know — it is Thomas who says,

"Lord, we do not know where you are going; how can we know the way?" (14:5). And when Jesus' friend Lazarus dies and Jesus tells his companions he must risk the hostility against him in the Jerusalem area by going to Lazarus's home, it is Thomas again who says to the rest of the group, in effect, "we might as well go with [Jesus] and die with him as well" (11:16).

It is the brief narrative about Thomas's encounter with Jesus after Jesus' resurrection that earns him the label of "the doubter." For some reason, according to John's account, Thomas was not present when Jesus appeared to his followers on the evening of his resurrection. (There is some unevenness in the post-resurrection accounts. Both Mark and Luke tell of an appearance to two followers who were not apostles which Matthew and John do not relate. In Matthew, Mark, and Luke, Jesus appears to all of the eleven remaining apostles at once; they apparently do not know the account of John that Thomas "was not with the rest when the Lord came" [20:24]. The one consistent fact in all four Gospel accounts is that either the news of Jesus' resurrection was first heard or his appearance first seen by women.) According to John, when Jesus' companions told him, "we have seen the Lord," Thomas was blunt in his response. "Unless I see the mark of the nails in his hand, unless I put my finger into the place where the nails were, and my hand into his side, I will not believe it" (20:25). Here is the honest skeptic, unwilling to accept someone else's word for what, on the face of it, would be an unbelievable account. Thomas wants proof that he himself can verify and he demands what in empirical terms would be considered a treble verification: he not only wants to see, with his own eyes, the marks of the nails driven into Jesus' hands, he wants to put his finger into those holes, as well as be able to thrust his hand into the place in Jesus' side where a soldier had thrust a spear.

All of this suggests that Thomas was among the "friends" of Jesus who, according to Luke's account, "had been standing at a distance" when Jesus was executed (23:49). He would then have witnessed not only the nailing of Jesus' body to the cross but also his stabbing by a soldier who had been ordered to hasten the executions of Jesus and the two thieves who were crucified with him. If Thomas had seen Jesus' death, he would certainly not be satisfied by anything less than his own determination that Jesus had somehow been restored to life.

Walter Russell Bowie, who taught homiletics at the Episcopal Theological Seminary in Virginia, notes that there are two kinds of doubt. One is rooted in cynicism, "the doubt that is the sour fruit of mean and careless living which is incapable of producing any sure convictions." But there is also, writes Bowie, "the doubt of utterly sincere and honest minds who will not say what they do not think, and who in their intellectual integrity will not pretend to build belief until they have for it a foundation of certain fact."[1] It is not always possible, of course, to achieve the certainty in life that Thomas sought in his insistence that he would not believe in the resurrection of Jesus unless he could satisfy himself empirically that the person claiming to be Jesus was the same man whom Thomas knew to have been physically mutilated during the course of his execution. But this is not the point! What matters in the story of Thomas is the same matter that is at stake in the story of Job. It is the Bible's recognition and acknowledgment of our capacity, as God's creation, to be uncertain or hesitant at times about either the intentions or the actions of the Creator.

A week later, according to John's account, Jesus appears to Thomas and invites him to carry out the very validation that Thomas had insisted would be necessary for him to believe that Jesus was alive. Thomas then became a believer, but it is important to note that when he was a doubter, he was not drummed out of the ranks of the apostles. This, perhaps, is the significance of the fact that the Gospel recounts that it was a full week after Thomas expressed his dubiousness about the resurrection stories that Jesus appeared to him. In the space of that week, there was ample time for the other ten apostles to decide that Thomas was an untrustworthy companion — that his skepticism was harmful to the cause, that anyone less than a totally convinced, unswervingly enthusiastic disciple would not be, in modern terminology, "a good fit" for the new movement. Perhaps the risen Lord himself might have determined not to waste time and effort on the doubtful and the hesitant; better to reassure the believers than to try to convince the skeptical.

But none of that happened. Instead, a week later (eight days, according to the King James translation) Jesus appeared. We will never know why Jesus waited such a long time to appear before Thomas. It must have been a period during which Thomas's doubt only deepened. There are no other recorded appearances of the risen Lord during this interim; no one, therefore, could echo the initial reports of Jesus' resurrection and challenge Thomas's skepticism. He must have grown increasingly sorrowful, not only about Jesus' death but also about what must have appeared to him as the hallucinations of his colleagues. To rush too quickly to Jesus' appearance to Thomas, therefore, is to miss a major portion of what this story wishes to convey. John says that Jesus invited Thomas to place his finger and his hand in the wounds, and apparently Thomas did, for he cried out "My Lord and my God." But before all this, Thomas had made clear that he would not accept such a tale without

1. Walter R. Bowie, "Exposition," in *Interpreter's Bible*, vol. 8 (New York: Abingdon-Cokesbury, 1952), p. 116.

some convincing proof; and, in the manner in which the Gospel account is written, the message is conveyed clearly that Thomas's doubt was not an act of disloyalty but an understandable quest for some degree of certainty in the midst of an incredible circumstance.

Those who would believe in God and, in the case of Christians, believe the man from Nazareth to be God's supreme messenger, are not asked to be unthinking, unquestioning, blindly acquiescent creatures who accept all sorts of implausible assertions about either God or Jesus because to do so is to "have faith." To the contrary, the Bible is the record of those who question God, like Job, and those who refuse to take someone else's word for God's acts, like Thomas. It is also the record of those who, like Peter, are not quite sure of themselves and who seem to be unable to make up their minds.

Peter

Why does Peter appear so prominently in the Christian Scriptures? Why, of the twelve principal followers of Jesus, is Peter's name constantly mentioned while we know very little about the others? Perhaps because Peter is so much like Christians down through the ages — full of zeal and enthusiasm for the cause he has joined, anxious to appear totally loyal and devoted to its leader, ready to defend Jesus with his life, but also capable of going back on his word and of not being steadfast whenever the circumstances become too demanding. Peter is everyone who has ever pledged commitment to a cause and then become uncertain or distracted or, for some other reason, come to have second thoughts either about the endeavor or about their ability or willingness to give themselves completely to it.

Peter is the most outspoken of all Jesus' followers. When Jesus begins to talk with his disciples about his impending death, it is Peter who rebukes Jesus — "such will never happen to you," Peter says. When Jesus says he is going away to a place that the disciples cannot follow, Peter says "Lord, I will lay down my life for you." When Jesus tells his disciples that they will all come to doubt him or "fall from [their] faith," it is Peter who boasts, "Everyone else may fall away but I won't" (Mark 14:27-29). Nevertheless, it is Peter who, after Jesus is betrayed by Judas and arrested, "follows him at a distance" (Matthew 26:58) and, when he is accused by a servant-girl of being one of Jesus' followers, curses and swears, "I do not know the man" (Mark 14:66-72).

There are two other critical incidents of doubt in Peter's career. The first can be found in the Gospel of John, which recounts that, after Jesus' burial, Mary of Magdala came to the tomb, found the stone had been moved from its entrance, and ran to Peter and another unnamed disciple (apparently John) to tell them that Jesus' body was missing. Peter and John return to the tomb, and Peter enters and sees the burial shroud folded neatly and lying to one side. Later that evening, when the disciples are huddled together somewhere "behind locked doors," Jesus appears to them and speaks with them. It was at this meeting, according to John's account, that Thomas was not present — but presumably Peter was. A week later, Jesus appears to Thomas and overcomes Thomas's skepticism. "Some time later," John states, Jesus "showed himself to his disciples once again, by the sea of Tiberias" (21:1). The circumstances of this appearance are interesting. Peter is there, along with at least three other apostles (Thomas and the two sons of Zebedee, James and John) and three other disciples (Nathaniel, whom we know to have been from Cana in Galilee, and two who are not named). Peter announces to the group that he is going fishing!

Now, it may be that too much should not be made of Peter's announcement. It is possibly the second week or even later after Jesus' first set of post-resurrection appearances, and perhaps Peter has begun to have second thoughts about what he thought he saw. But more pertinent, Peter is a fisherman; perhaps he feels the need to get back to earning a livelihood, or it may be that fishing seemed like a good way to take his mind off the confusing jumble of events of the past few weeks.

Whatever the circumstances, is it nevertheless not just a bit startling — if not dismaying — to find Peter announcing that he is going fishing? It is Peter, after all, who, according to John's account, was the first to enter the tomb and find Jesus' body missing, with the grave cloths wrapped and laid to one side. Peter was among the ten who were gathered that same evening when Jesus appeared to the entire group (with the exception of Thomas). Would not one expect to find Peter — the one who had said, "others may fall away but I won't" — overwhelmed by the fact that Jesus was once again with his disciples? Wouldn't one expect him to be fired with eagerness to resume the mission for which Jesus had commissioned the twelve? Why do we find Peter announcing instead that he is returning to his old pursuit?

We find this because, in at least one respect, Peter is running true to form! This is the man whose life vacillates between affirmation and denial, between certainty and hesitation, between cocksuredness and faintheartedness, between faith and doubt. It can be considered either surprising or disappointing that Peter is a man of such inconstancy. That Peter's very name means "rock" almost seems a bad joke given his wavering record of instability. It is rather astonishing that he comes to play such a large leadership role in the life of the young church; one might expect a person of much more internal strength and firmness to take charge of the fledgling new movement. Somehow, however, Peter is entrusted with the responsibility of spokesperson for what was called "The Way." It is Peter who preaches the sermon on Pentecost when the first group of converts beyond the apostles themselves is added to the roster of Jesus' disciples; it is Peter who begins to display the gift of healing (Acts 3:1-10) and who emerges as the leader of the remaining apostles (4:5-9). We are given the clear impression, in these post-resurrection accounts and in the stories of the first days of the Christian movement, that the man on whom the earliest organizational and evangelical efforts of the church depended was someone who himself had displayed all the doubts and misgivings that any potential adherent of the movement might face. At its very outset, therefore, the message appears to be that the arms of the church are open the widest to those who are least sure of its proclamation.

The second critical incident of doubt in Peter's career is the more significant, for it has far more long-term implications for the life of the Christian community, up to and including — perhaps especially — our own time. To understand this incident, we must remember that the first Christians were all good Jews. "The Way" was initially seen by both its advocates and its opponents as a movement within Judaism whose followers had become convinced that Jesus of Nazareth was the long-awaited Jewish Messiah. One of the earliest and most enduring controversies in the early church, therefore, was whether Jewish followers of the Way (or Christianity) should continue to behave as good, practicing Jews, distinguished only by the fact that they believed the Messiah of God had finally come in the presence of Jesus the Anointed of God.

The spokesperson for this latter position — that Christians were Jews who believed Jesus to be the Messiah and who, in all other respects, were to continue to observe their religious commitments and obligations as practicing Jews — was James, leader of the group of Christians in Jerusalem and none other than Jesus' brother (a fact that undoubtedly gave him some added status, both in the community and in the ensuing controversy). Paul, who had not as yet come on the scene, would emerge as the powerful spokesman for an alternative view of this matter. Poor Peter, as might be expected, found himself right in the middle of the dispute!

Peter began as a firm advocate of the position that Christians were Jews who claimed Jesus as the Messiah of God. He insisted, together with James and the other leaders of the fledgling church in Jerusalem, that in all essential respects, these new followers of Jesus had to observe all the ritual requirements of Judaism — circumcision for males, observance of the Sabbath for worship, and maintaining kosher dietary laws. The Way, therefore, was seen as a reform movement within Judaism, not a brand new religion.

With Paul's conversion and his growing conviction that the Christian movement ought to be as open to non-Jews as it was to Jews, the scene was set for a major clash with Paul and his followers on one side and the leaders of the church in Jerusalem under the leadership of James on the other. It is in the midst of this controversy that the fascinating incident recorded in the tenth chapter of the book of Acts occurs.

Peter has just completed a general tour of the new churches and has stopped in Joppa when, in Caesarea, a coastal town to the north, a Roman military commander named Cornelius has a vision in which he is told to send for Peter. The following day, Peter falls into a trance in which he sees a large sheet being lowered from heaven with all sorts of creatures on it, "whatever walks or crawls or flies" (10:9-16). While Peter is trying to figure out what this heavenly scene means, messengers from Cornelius arrive and ask Peter to accompany them to Caesarea, which he does; when he meets Cornelius, who is not a Jew, the meaning of the trance becomes clear to Peter. "I now see," Peter states, "how true it is that God has no favorites but that in every nation the man who is god-fearing and does what is right is acceptable to him" (10:34). We have, therefore, in this story, the first confrontation of a church whose members were all Jews with the reality that the church's mission and message were meant for a much wider audience.

When Peter subsequently returns to Jerusalem he is confronted by James and his colleagues, who have apparently heard of Peter's encounter with Cornelius. Peter repeats the story of his vision and, we are told, when the Jerusalem congregation "heard this their doubts were silenced. They gave praise to God and said, 'This means that God has granted life-giving repentance to the Gentiles also'" (11:18).

It is, on its face, a beautiful story about the openness and inclusiveness of the Christian gospel and the Christian faith, and it would be one of the great moments in the life of the church were it not for a rather sad epilogue. Some years later, Paul recounts making a trip to Jerusalem where he met with the leaders of the Jerusalem church and where the dispute over the terms of admission of non-Jews to the Christian fold was still raging. Paul describes working out an agreement with the Jerusalem leaders (he specifically mentions James, Peter, and John) in which Paul was commissioned to carry the church's message to non-Jews while the Jerusalem group would continue seeking to convert Jews. It was made a matter of record; Paul says they "shook hands on it" (Galatians 2:9). But then Paul tells of a subsequent visit of Peter to Antioch in which Peter was perfectly content to meet with the Christians there who were not Jews, until several emissaries from James arrived, whereupon Peter "drew back and began to hold aloof" because he feared those who were still insisting on circumcision as a requirement for the admission of non-Jews to the Christian fold (2:12). And Paul states, "I opposed Peter to his face, because he was clearly in the wrong" (2:11).

It is, regrettably, yet one more instance of Peter's doubtfulness — in this case, doubting the validity of the message that he had been given in the vision he experienced just before his trip to Cornelius. At first he understood the meaning of the vision perfectly — even eloquently, as he relates its significance to Cornelius and his relatives, and as he must have conveyed it to the leaders of the church in Jerusalem. But when he is back in his old haunts and with his old comrades, Peter becomes uncertain about whether he should risk the disapproval of those who think the gospel of Jesus was meant only for Jewish ears. And so he does what one who lacks conviction would do: he readily eats with non-Jewish Christians when his orthodox Jerusalem cronies are not around but withdraws from their midst when the Jerusalem brethren appear. James might well have had Peter in mind when he later wrote that "a double-minded man is unstable in all his ways" (James 1:8).

It must be acknowledged with considerable sorrow that if Peter did not get the message, neither have those who have followed in his footsteps over the course of the past two millennia. The tragic thread that runs through the history of the church up to and including the present time is one in which the church continuously faces — and more often than not succumbs to — the temptation to think of itself in exclusive, rather than inclusive, terms.

In one sense, this is a problem with every community, however that community defines and draws its boundaries. Whether the line of demarcation is nationality, race, ethnicity, social or sexual status, or any other criterion, what begins as a way of identifying the community becomes, either quickly or over time, a barrier to keep others out. Every form of human community, from neighborhood to nation, is erected on this premise and process, and many of the world's woes come from its persistence.

So ubiquitous is this phenomenon that we might mistakenly think it is part of the natural order of the universe. It is not. Building exclusive communities is a human preference, not a social necessity. Much less is it a divine desire or command. Instead, it occurs among people who lack the maturity and self-confidence to embrace a wider world than they would ordinarily find comfortable and comforting.

The church was intended, in part, as a new form of human community that would overcome these artificial boundaries. This was Paul's repeated message: God has made of one blood all nations that dwell on the face of the earth; there is one body and one spirit, as there is one hope; in Christ, you are neither Jew nor Greek, male nor female, slave nor free. The church was to reflect a broader truth and a wider reality, a new creation of Christ's that would transcend human divisions and separations.

Instead, the church has been a mirror of the world's smaller, narrower prejudices. To their everlasting shame, vast segments of the church revel in its differences, applauding the fact that people find comfort, identity, and spiritual renewal in congregations, denominations, and national churches that represent the same narrow interests, visions, and associations that mark the rest of their lives. That the world is marred by conflict rooted in the artificialities of ethnicity, race, nation, and ideology should not be surprising given the fact that the church has not found it possible — and sadly, in many quarters, even necessary — to overcome these sins. This marks the church as a community plagued by something far worse than skepticism — a disbelief in the essential mission and message of its Lord whose last prayer was that his disciples would be one community of believers.

We should feel compassion for Peter, then, because he is so much like us; and, when faced with temptations toward exclusiveness in the church, we should remember the vision God sent him. But we should also pray for the courage of Job, who did not shrink from arguing with God about the absence of justice and equity in the world. And we could benefit from the skepticism of Thomas, especially in the face of the modern world's peddlers of faith, who offer all sorts of spiritual nostrums in the name of Christ. Taken together, these three mortals suggest a model of faith that is hammered out on the anvil of questioning, thoughtful reflection, and discernment. Nothing less is worthy of God.

Chapter 7

Through a Glass Darkly

Near the end of his first letter to the church in Corinth, Paul engages in an extended discussion of resurrection and immortality. The discussion is remarkable for its intricate detail. After taking note of Jesus' resurrection and the numerous witnesses to that event, Paul takes up the challenge of those who do not believe that the dead can be resurrected, arguing somewhat circularly that if there is no such thing as resurrection then not only have all who have died indeed perished, but believers in the resurrection cling to a hope that has no possibility of fulfillment and Paul and the others who have testified to Christ's resurrection are false witnesses.

Paul then proceeds to describe what commentaries on this passage call the "eschatological drama" or the sequence of events that is to occur at the end of time. He contrasts the temporary nature of life in this world and its inevitable end in death — as symbolized by Adam — with the immortality that is symbolized by and awaits believers in Christ. He then depicts "the end" as a period of messianic reign by Jesus which is apparently to precede the final judgment.

There follows a quite specific discussion of the nature of the resurrection in which Paul gives his answer to the question, "With what kind of body do the dead come forth?" Here, it is apparent that Paul does not wish to encourage a belief in the resurrection of our physical body. In fact, he denies that such will occur and instead declares that in the resurrection we will be given a spiritual body, a form quite distinct from that of our earthly existence. And then comes Paul's dramatic declaration that is captured so magnificently by Handel in his beloved oratorio *The Messiah*: "Behold, I tell you a mystery. We shall not all sleep, but we shall all be changed . . . for the trumpet will sound and the dead will be raised imperishable. . . ." Death and the grave will have been, in Paul's words, "swallowed up in victory," a victory that has been given through "our Lord Jesus Christ" (1 Corinthians 15:54-57).

The entire account is remarkable for its precision and specificity. Paul writes with obvious confidence, and his affirmations seem calculated to allay any doubt or confusion among those who hear him about the subjects of the resurrection and immortality. Earlier, however, in this same letter and in the midst of an oft-quoted passage on love, Paul made this curious assertion: "for now we see through a glass darkly, but then face to face" (1 Corinthians 13:12). Here, confident proclamations about the end times and the life of the world to come are absent. There are no soaring descriptions of the manner in which the mortal realm ceases and the immortal reign begins. Instead, there is the poignant observation that certainty about things eternal is not possible for us mortals. In this life, Paul seems to say, we have the ability to grasp or sense obliquely what will become clear only in the world to come.

After reading these two passages, we are left with at least two questions. First, why is Paul so certain and precise about the afterlife in one passage while cautioning against — indeed, almost denying the validity of — his certainness in another? Does he forget what he has written earlier or is he simply indifferent to the obvious contradictions between his two statements? And why, in the earlier passage, does he depart from a moving discourse on love — its making and meaning — to speak of the veil that keeps us from seeing clearly the life to come?

There is an obvious and irreconcilable inconsistency in these two statements of Paul, the one which speaks so assuredly about features of the next world and the other which acknowledges that such knowledge is not possible. In one respect, however, the inconsistency is troublesome only for those who expect Scripture to provide an unfailingly accurate account of every matter it addresses and who value consistency and uniformity above spiritual truth. Paul himself must have been aware of the clash between the ideas that these two passages present; after all, they appear in the same letter! It is not as though he wrote in a later epistle thoughts that conflicted with what he had written in earlier correspondence. Precisely because the two passages appear in the same letter, we have to deal with their contradictions. Why would Paul send two such distinctly different and incongruous messages to the same group of congregants, especially when some among them were apparently doubtful about the whole idea of a resurrection in the first place?

A clue to Paul's thinking may be found in the passage cited earlier: "Behold, I tell you a mystery. . . ." Paul is fond of this term "mystery," particularly in this Corinthian letter; he speaks of the mystery of God's wisdom (2:7), of ministers as "stewards of God's mysteries" (4:1), and of the irrelevance of understanding mysteries if one does not possess love (13:2). For Paul, a mystery seems to be some insight into the mind of God, some wisdom that has been hidden but is revealed and, as Paul believes, becomes accessible to everyone who would reach out for it.

Paul is, in this regard, at one with those down through the ages who have pointed to those experiences or insights in life that, either at the moment or upon later reflection, have a spiritual meaning that is not apparent to the senses or obvious to the intellect. Thus the term "mystery" has long pointed to that which cannot be fully understood by rational analysis — that which is apprehended as real but which also baffles or perplexes the mind and confounds ordinary, sensate experience. It is a pity that the idea of mystery has been degraded in modern thought to become virtually synonymous with the detective story. There is this far older and richer use of the term that connotes those moments in which mortals contemplate their relationship to the total universe and perceive that universe as an expanse that extends far beyond, as well as transcends, their ability to grasp it.

It is but a short step from mystery to mystics and mysticism. Mystics and mysticism have not been as readily acknowledged and welcomed in the ranks of Christianity as they have been in Hinduism and Buddhism, and far less by Protestants than by Roman Catholics and the Eastern Orthodox. The idea of direct communication with God — the belief that one can have direct knowledge of God or of spiritual truth through subjective, personal experiences, a belief at the heart of mysticism and the mystical ideal — flies in the face of much of traditional Christian teaching about the nature of divine revelation. But if mystery points to that which cannot be fully understood, that which baffles and perplexes and especially that which cannot be grasped by the senses, if the mystical is that which has a spiritual meaning that is neither apparent to the senses nor obvious to the intellect, and if the mystic is one who speaks of such knowledge and experiences, then Paul is foremost among Christian mystics!

Albert Schweitzer, renowned for his life as a medical missionary in Africa, was also a New Testament scholar of considerable note. Among his major writings is a book entitled *The Mysticism of Paul the Apostle.* In Schweitzer's view,

> whenever in the great thinkers or under the influence of great movements of thought Christianity endeavors to attain to clarity regarding the relation of God and the world, it cannot help opening the doors to

> mysticism. . . . We are always in the presence of mysticism when we find a human being looking upon the division between earthly and super-earthly, temporal and eternal . . . and feeling himself, while still externally amid the earthly and the temporal, to belong to the super-earthly and the eternal.[1]

Nothing better describes the mind that Paul seems to possess or to be possessed by in his first letter to the Corinthians. And the mystical experience is not confined to this one incident for Paul. In his second Corinthian letter, he speaks enigmatically of being "caught up to the third heaven," taken "into Paradise" (2 Corinthians 12:2, 3). Elsewhere Paul writes with carefully structured arguments and systematically presents his case for Christianity, but when he discourses on the resurrection, Paul confronts a spiritual truth that he realizes undoubtedly will be puzzling and difficult for others to comprehend. It is certainly one that Paul knows is not grasped by the processes of logic and rational thought. Thus Paul declares it to be a *mystery* — a spiritual truth not obvious to the senses and one that defies human reason.

So persuaded is he of the reality of Jesus' resurrection that Paul is anxious for everyone to understand its significance, which, for Paul, lies in the fact that death has lost its power to threaten humankind with ultimate annihilation. So Paul finds himself describing this mystery in exquisite detail — the end of this mortal era, the messianic reign of Jesus, the resurrection of the dead, and their final judgment. He is, in such a moment, the mystic who feels himself, in Schweitzer's words, "while still externally amid the earthly and the temporal, to belong to the super-earthly and the eternal." Paul has been permitted to glimpse the life beyond this life and seeks, in the language of the mystic, to convince others of its reality.

But Paul the mystic is also Paul who was once a Pharisee. He is used to marshaling his arguments with precision and presenting his case with reasoned care. He goes to great lengths, as one commentator states, "to find points of contact with his hearers' ways of thinking."[2] As his encounter with the Stoics and Epicureans in Athens demonstrates (Acts 17), Paul respects the life of the mind and the demands of making a persuasive intellectual argument. In such a mode in his famous encounter on Mars Hill, he tries unsuccessfully to convince the Athenian philosophers of the reality of the resurrection. Having failed to do so, he seems to acknowledge in his statement about

1. Albert Schweitzer, *The Mysticism of Paul the Apostle* (New York: Seabury, 1968), pp. 1-2.

2. Theodore Ferris, "Exposition of Acts," in *The Interpreter's Bible*, ed. George Arthur Buttrick et al., 12 vols. (New York: Abingdon-Cokesbury, 1951-57), vol. 9, p. 232.

"seeing through a glass darkly" that his understanding of things eternal is, in the final analysis, a truth that is only dimly and mystically perceived.

It may have been his failure in Athens, in fact, that ultimately convinced Paul of the futility of rational arguments about the resurrection. Athens is widely acknowledged to be one of the few places where Paul's message did not attract a significant following; it is one of the few major cities where he did not establish a congregation. His description of the resurrection as a mystery may indicate his realization that the things pertaining to the life beyond can be conveyed and received only as spiritual — not as rational — truths.

There is one other observation that may help to explain Paul's contradictory assertions. Paul always readily admits that which many Christian believers down through the centuries have found it difficult to acknowledge about him: Paul is human. Whatever inspiration drove him to pen his letters to various congregations and to three of his close associates, he still considers himself "the least of the apostles" (1 Corinthians 15:9), indicates that he feels "perplexed" when some of his efforts go awry (2 Corinthians 4:8), acknowledges his timidity in the face of the task of preaching (1 Corinthians 2:3), and expresses his human frailty in the poignant phrase "O wretched man that I am" (Romans 7:24). When he speaks of "seeing through a glass darkly," therefore, he may only be stating what is the fundamental realization of every believer — that the future lies not in human understanding but in the hands of God. We who are but mere mortals may anticipate that future, but precisely because it transcends this realm and existence we cannot know its form or substance.

We still are left with the peculiar fact that Paul acknowledges the limits of his human capacity to grasp the eternal in a passage in which his thought is riveted on love and its immense possibilities. Why interrupt such a sublime rumination about the transforming power of love with a brief but discursive reflection on the limits of human knowledge? As it turns out, the discursive interruption may not be as out of place as it seems. It may, in fact, be an integral part of the point that Paul wishes to make.

Paul's fundamental point is that love is eternal. He wishes his readers to understand that while everything else in this mortal realm lacks permanence or can be transitory, love is unending and unfailing. All the positions, skills, and virtues that members of the Corinthian church prided themselves in possessing — the posts of teachers, healers, and prophets, the ability to speak in tongues and work miracles — all this, says Paul, is of no value whatever when compared with the capacity to love and to participate in its enduring power. And it is in this context — of discussing the eternal characteristics of love and its absolute superiority to every other type or dimension of human experience — that Paul reflects on the limitations of human knowledge.

In contrast to the permanence of love, Paul declares that knowledge — like the ability to prophesy and to speak in tongues — will "pass away." To us moderns, Paul combines a peculiar trinity of talents to make his point. Prophecy has not been practiced in Christian circles for centuries and speaking in tongues is considered in most quarters of the Christian church to be a quaint ritual found only among some Pentecostal groups. Knowledge, however, is at the heart of the human enterprise and is integral to the Christian experience; why would Paul dare to suggest that it, too, is as impermanent as the ability to prophesy or to speak in tongues?

While we may not wish to attribute to Paul the insights about knowledge of which we are capable two thousand years later, we are aware of how rapidly knowledge can become obsolete — of the obsolescence of much of the knowledge of a century or even a decade ago. The universe of knowledge is a steadily expanding enterprise. It is constantly subject to change and revision. In this sense, Paul is right that old forms of knowledge "pass away" as newer discoveries and fresh insights are made.

But this does not seem to be what Paul has in mind. His is the insight that all of the knowledge we humans can attain is limited by our own humanness. Paul's assertion reminds us of our creatureliness; all the knowledge of which we are capable as humans is knowledge limited by the fact that it is the effort and the outcome of human endeavor — and humans, as much as it may pain us to admit as much, are finite creatures. Accordingly, our knowledge is finite and forever subject to the limitations of our finite minds and world. This is why, Paul says, we "see through a glass darkly" or, as the Revised Standard Version translates it, "in a mirror dimly." We see dimly because, Paul insists, we can as mortals know only "in part"; our knowledge is restricted to the realm we inhabit and cannot possibly extend to that sphere which is beyond our own frame of existence. But there will come a time, declares Paul, when we will understand fully, even as we are fully understood by God.

If this is so, why does Paul proceed, later in the letter, to do what he says is impossible to do — to describe and depict that which he admits is beyond human description? There are two possibilities, one of which Paul himself indicates; about the other we may only speculate. To understand the first possibility, we must remember that in the passage in which he sets forth his vision of the end time and the nature of the resurrection, Paul is explicit in alerting his readers that he speaks as a mystic: "Behold, I tell you a mystery." Paul puts himself on record as presenting a perspective on things to come that cannot be grasped by the conventional tools of human intelligence; it is not a rational view of the life beyond this realm but one which Paul, although he is duly modest about it, has been privileged to glimpse because he is part of a special group of believers. He numbers himself among the company of the apostles, although he considers himself one "born out of due season" and unfit to be called an apostle (1 Corinthians 15:8). Nevertheless, as one of the eyewitnesses to Jesus' resurrection, Paul believes that his is a special status, one accompanied by special insights, among which is the mystery he shares with the Corinthian congregation regarding the resurrection.

It is also possible, however, that there is a much simpler explanation for Paul's seemingly confusing assertions, an explanation that anyone can easily understand, if not affirm. Each of us, at some point or points in our life, has faced the urge or temptation to put into words that which cannot be articulated, to express the inexpressible and give verbal substance to an experience or an insight that we realize lies beyond our capacity to depict or describe. I have known such moments viewing a range of mountains or standing inside a cathedral or in the bliss of an especial intimacy. That which I know I cannot put into words I nevertheless strive to. There is something irrepressible in the human psyche that feels compelled to give verbal definition to everything we encounter that has meaning for us. Perhaps this need to verbalize our most significant and cherished experiences is not surprising; speaking is, after all, the primary way in which we communicate with others. The more complex the experience, the more we rely on our verbal skills in the attempt to express its significance.

So Paul may have simply succumbed to that instinct embedded in each of us to try to imagine — to form a mental image of, in the literal sense of the word — that which was not part of his world and which lay beyond his experience and his ability, as well as ours, to fully understand. Paul may have done what countless men and women before and since have also sought to do, to give shape and substance to that which must always remain a hope and an expectation beyond our ability to grasp or fully comprehend.

It seems clear, therefore, that much of what I might strive to know and understand about the hereafter is beyond my human capacity to understand. This leaves me vulnerable to the cynics, who can declare that mine is the intellectually cheap or easy response of those who say, in the final analysis, "it is all a matter of faith." But I believe there is something more here: the recognition and acceptance of the limitations of my own ability to fully perceive that which, by definition, is beyond the realm of human experience and thus of human comprehension.

I could, of course, decide that I will simply not concern myself with that which is beyond my ability to apprehend. Something within me resists this, however, as the intellectually cheap and easy way out of my quandary. As Paul states at the beginning of his meditation on love, surely there is "a more excellent way."

Chapter 8

Immortality and Its Alternative

Why is it not possible, at the end of one's life, simply to acknowledge that one's existence on this earth has been good and sufficient in itself — that living has been its own reward — and not expect anything more? Why not be content with whatever joys and satisfactions we manage to experience in this world — our family, work, friends, the possessions we acquire and use, the adventures we pursue? Why not look back on these moments and memories with a sense of gratitude and fulfillment and consider it enough? Why do we mortals become caught up in the notion that there is something else awaiting us, beyond the life we have already received and enjoyed?

Not everyone, in fact, is driven by such an idea. In every age there are those for whom the assumed attractiveness of immortality has no appeal. Some reject as wishful thinking the notion that life, with all the fragileness and uncertainty it displays in this earthly realm, somehow becomes permanent and unending in some other sphere. Others scoff at the idea of being either rewarded or punished in a life to come for one's behavior in this life. Still others find the arguments for an afterlife to be totally at odds with the mountains of evidence with which we are confronted every day of our existence.

Perhaps no one has better stated the case for these latter points of view than two of antiquity's most revered philosophers: Epicurus, who lived between 341 and 270 B.C., and Lucretius, whose life spanned the years 99 to 55 B.C. The fact that Lucretius preceded the birth of Jesus of Nazareth by only a half-century or so adds a certain irony to the fact he, together with Epicurus, articulated a view of life so radically different from that which Jesus espoused.

Epicurus grappled with the problem of how we mortals can get beyond life's uncertainties and live with contentment in what is obviously a disorderly world. Resolving this dilemma was crucial for Epicurus precisely because, in his view, we have only one life to live and have to make the best of it. Accordingly, his goal was to promote happiness and to avoid or make himself free from pain, trouble, and, especially, fear, the greatest fear being the fear of death and what would happen after it. In fact, Epicurus sought to promote happiness *by* avoiding these things, since he believed that happiness, or pleasure, could be defined as the absence of pain. The more pleasure we experience, the better the life; the more pain, the worse the life. A life of asceticism based on the reduction of desire to an absolute minimum was therefore the path to pleasure, to absolute freedom from pain, and to unbroken tranquility. It is for this reason that Epicurus's principal aim has been described as "the search for imperturbability — the asset that renders the wise [person] entirely independent of the vicissitudes of fortune and . . . all forces outside of [oneself]."[1] The happy life is not one of physical pleasure alone but also, and to a greater degree, one of a tranquil mind. Accordingly, Epicurus counsels, the wise person will not fall in love, marry, or raise a family. Instead, he or she will feel gratitude toward friends, avoid politics, not become a mendicant, and not commit suicide. All of this is to avoid trouble and should lead to a sense of well-being.

Two centuries later Lucretius, drawing heavily on Epicurus, set out a markedly similar set of views. Lucretius taught that

> creation and the life of man [is] a pure accident, having no significance beyond itself; . . . nature [is] neither kindly nor hostile to us, but indifferent; and . . . the only sensible purpose of living [is] to attain, through well-spaced and well-chosen pleasures and an intelligent understanding of the universe, a calm and reassured happiness.[2]

Beneath this sentiment lay what was, for its time, a sophisticated scientific analysis, which Lucretius set forth in his major work, *De Rerum Natura* (On the Nature of Things). Lucretius acknowledged that humankind's greatest fear is the fear of death and possible punishment in the hereafter, but he claimed that such fears are needless. The world, he argued, is composed of atoms that are infinite and eternal. Because death is the dissolution of the atomic structure that is human life, it should be of no particular concern. "No thing," he wrote, "relapses into non-existence, but all things at dissolution return to the first principles of matter [i.e., the primordial elements or atoms] that are infinite and eternal."[3]

1. Michael Grant, *Greek and Latin Authors* (New York: H. W. Wilson, 1980), p. 145.

2. Gilbert Highet, *The Classical Tradition* (New York: Oxford University Press, 1957), p. 433.

3. Quoted in Robert Beck, *Perspectives in Philosophy* (New York: Holt, Rinehart and Winston, 1961), pp. 154-55.

Human life as we know it, therefore, dissolves and decays into the basic, atomic elements of which it is composed; the structure of human existence ceases but its substance remains indestructible.

Neither Epicurus nor Lucretius believed in an afterlife. Epicurus simply argued that the gods were "too remote and too happy to meddle with earthly matters and that the art of living should not be distorted by such wild imaginations" as belief in a future existence.[4] Lucretius joined him in the conviction that the gods "had nothing to do with the world."[5] For Lucretius, the soul "comes to life with the body, grows with the body, and dies with the body, so that in old age, just as one would expect, judgment falters and speech and thought both wander; the old age of the body is the beginning of the death of all we are."[6]

In Epicurean thought, then, we find this sharp distinction between the human and the divine realms. While the basic elements of the human sphere (i.e., atoms) may be eternal and indestructible, their composition in human form is not. Human life is as transitory and subject to decay as are all life forms in the universe. The Christian belief that, in Paul's words, we mortals who are subject to corruptibility or decay will put on or "be clothed in" immortality and incorruptibility is not only absent from but totally alien to Epicurean thought.

It should not be supposed that Epicurus and those who expressed similar views were self-centered pleasure-seekers living debauched lives of indifference or disdain toward others or toward the society around them. Epicurus is described as a person who "spoke gently, gave alms to the poor, and preached against wealth, ambition, [and] passion."[7] Horace, the Roman poet whose writings reflect Epicurean views, was an advocate "of the simple life, of contentment with moderate means, of philosophic calm and of the golden mean," the ancient ideal of measured moderation in all of living.[8]

At the least, therefore, one must acknowledge that many of the virtues the Epicureans espoused are praiseworthy. Pursuing the simple life, giving to the poor, and being moderate in one's tastes and endeavors are laudable principles for anyone to follow. Some of the Epicurean admonitions, such as advising against falling in love and marriage, may seem a bit problematic (al-

4. Melvin Rader, *The Enduring Questions* (New York: Henry Holt, 1956), p. 211.

5. Highet, *Classical Tradition,* p. 421.

6. Jay W. Hudson, *The Truths We Live By* (New York: D. Appleton, 1930), pp. 123-24.

7. Rader, *Enduring Questions,* p. 211.

8. Casper J. Kraemer Jr., ed., *The Complete Works of Horace* (New York: Modern Library, 1936), p. ix.

though there are dozens of modern novels testifying to the fact that both acts are as filled with the potential for misery and disappointment as they are with the potential for happiness). Similarly, avoiding politics would not generally be considered a way of fostering civic commitment and a sense of public responsibility. Both admonitions are radically inconsistent with current calls in America for restoring family values or seizing the reins of government in order to rebuild the moral fiber of the nation. But the emphasis on gratitude, on the importance of friendships, and on the value of happiness is not to be quarreled with, at least from a Christian point of view.

Nor can one find fault with the desire to find a way to live contentedly in a disordered world. Everywhere one turns these days, various formulae and recipes are being offered — new age, meditative, psychological, psychedelic, and spiritual — as ways to transcend the uncertainties and disappointments of life and achieve an inner calm. For Epicurean thought to suggest that one way of doing so is by freeing ourselves of certain illusions, by concentrating our attention and our energies on that which is pleasurable, and by avoiding pain as much as possible while maximizing opportunities for happiness in our lives is not advice to be dismissed out of hand.

Whether belief in an afterlife is an illusion is a matter to which we must turn momentarily. What is initially suspect in Epicurean thought, however, is its emphasis on happiness as the primary, if not the exclusive, aim of human existence. The problem is not so much that happiness as a goal in life is improper or inappropriate but that it is, for Epicureans, so singular an aim. One suspects, in fact, that the followers of Epicureanism are likely to be people like the farmer in one of Jesus' parables who wanted to build bigger barns in which to store his exceptional harvest — wealthy people for whom most aspects of life have fallen comfortably into place, as is often the case for the affluent. For such persons, pursuing the pleasurable and seeking happiness frequently becomes a way of life in itself. It is difficult, however, to imagine a person who receives a layoff notice at his or her place of employment, or who is trying to raise a family on income from a minimum-wage job, or whose life is consumed by the care of an aged parent or a disabled child, finding much solace in the idea that happiness is the chief aim or end in life.

It is even more difficult to envision those to whom life brings unexpected, unremitting, and unavoidable pain as having much patience with the idea of living as an adventure in happiness-seeking. Pain comes in many forms in life — mental, physical, and spiritual — at unexpected times and in totally unanticipated ways. Some individuals suffer from emotional or spiritual agonies, and they have their own private journeys through hell with which to deal. Less unexpected, perhaps, but no less welcome is physical pain.

It is almost a given that pain accompanies the process of aging; unusual and exceptionally fortunate are those who reach retirement age without experiencing some difficulty that manifests itself in persistent physical discomfort. The pain found in various forms of cancer or other diseases for which there is either no known cure or the chances of survival are poor is likely the least explicable of all of life's tragic experiences, especially when it befalls a child or those who are thought to be in the prime of life. Persons in such circumstances might earnestly wish for happiness and contentment; with Epicurus, they may devoutly desire to avoid pain. But as far too many people can attest, pain cannot be overcome in every circumstance as an act of the will. Avoiding it may require many other means than the sheer effort to do so, and often those other means are of no avail.

Given the reality of pain as an inevitable part of human existence, the important question becomes how we shall confront and deal with it. We can seek to ignore pain whenever possible, we can determine to face it and its causes stoically, we can seek remedies or therapies if they are available, or we can try to discover some deeper meaning or purpose in an experience that, in most cases, seems to be devoid of any rational explanation. It is part of the human condition to search for answers in every confounding situation we face. However we conceive of ourselves and our origins, it would betray the innermost sense of who we are and what we are as human creatures simply to accept life and whatever it brings, as though we were mindless robots unable to ponder or question our fate. So it is, even with pain. However else we deal with it, we almost always press for causes and search for reasons; we demand to know *why,* even in those utterly distressing situations in which there are no organic or logical or reasonable answers.

Epicurean thought, therefore, seems to fall short as a philosophy of life, other than, perhaps, for the very well-to-do who have everything this life can offer, or the young and carefree for whom there are no significant life stresses, for whom life constitutes one unending joyride. And the young — although they may imagine themselves immune from life's inexorabilities — grow into middle and old age, and the well-to-do must still face all the uncertainties of life, including the market's capacity to plunge one's hopes and plans into a financial tailspin.

But what shall we say about the Epicurean view of an afterlife, or, rather, of its denial that such is a possibility? It is here that Epicurean and Christian thought clash irreconcilably. A philosophy, as one observer notes,

> which postulated a wholly material and mechanistic universe shaped without divine participation, which denied the gods a providential

> role in the affairs of mankind, and which looked to pleasure as the first and ultimate goal of human existence would seem to stand at variance with the very fundamentals of Christian teaching.[9]

It is here, therefore, as so often happens in life when clear alternatives present themselves, that one must make a choice. It is possible to lead a perfectly respectable — indeed admirable — existence without any expectation that there is yet another life beyond this mortal plane. I have a number of friends who do not believe in immortality or a life beyond the one we lead on this earth. They are loving, generous, thoughtful, considerate human beings whose lives make it difficult to support the view of those who argue that it is only a fear of punishment or the hope of a reward in the next world that makes us lead decent lives in this one. At the same time, I am not so sure that I would conduct my own life as I have tried to if it were not for the feeling that somehow, somewhere other than in this existence, I will be held accountable for myself. I can speak best about myself, and I suspect that I would be a bit less tolerant on occasion, less charitable or less understanding, and more inclined to think of my own needs and wishes (than I already am!) if I did not think that I will have to answer for myself.

Two fathers of the early church wrestled with this dilemma. One, Gregory of Nyssa, asked, "how can virtue have a place among those who hold that this present life is the total sum of existence and that beyond it nothing is to be looked for?"[10] My friends who do live virtuous lives but who do not believe in immortality seem to indicate that it is possible. But I have the feeling that they are exceptions to the general rule, and that Athenagoras got it right when he wrote,

> For if no judgment whatever were to be passed on the actions of men . . . a life after the manner of brutes would be the best, virtue would be absurd, the threat of judgment a matter for broad laughter, indulgence in every kind of pleasure the highest good, and the common resolve of all these [the Epicureans] and their one law would be that maxim, so dear to the intemperate and lewd, "let us eat and drink, for tomorrow we die."[11]

I also do not see enough of due recompense in the world, either for good or evil, to be content with the idea that the scales are somehow balanced in

9. Howard Jones, *The Epicurean Tradition* (London: Routledge, 1989), p. 96.
10. Quoted in Jones, *Epicurean Tradition*, p. 100.
11. Quoted in Jones, *Epicurean Tradition*, pp. 100-101.

this life. The lament of the Psalmist — "why do the evil prosper?" — is the outcry of many, myself included, who consider this life a cruel hoax if its rewards and punishments are being distributed according to some norm or standard that supposedly equates with fairness or justice. Essential to life, it seems to me, at least, is some sense that its outcomes are more than just the result of caprice or happenstance — that the daily instances of greed, cruelty, and harmfulness reported by the media are not signs of "the way life is" but rather the way things ought not to be. There is little reason to struggle against the insanity of this world if, in the end, our struggles really matter little (if at all) as to the outcome. If that is the case, then the cynicism of the writer of Ecclesiastes is quite apt: "vanity of vanities, everything is in vain."

Somehow, I find more realistic the parable that Jesus tells regarding the man whose attitude would seem to mirror at least some Epicurean beliefs.[12] As Jesus recounts it (in Luke 12:16-21), life has been good to this man. His fields have been fertile and his harvests plentiful — so much so that he lacks sufficient storage for his crops. Contemplating his situation, he determines to tear down his old barns and build newer, larger ones. (Whether he is motivated by greed or prudence is unclear.)[13] With this accomplished he could say to himself, "soul, relax; eat, drink, and enjoy yourself" — the perfect Epicurean mantra. To which God responds, "Fool, this night your soul will be required of you; then whose will those things be which you have provided?"

It is of more than passing interest that the central figure in this story has this dialogue with his soul, not with his heirs or his financial planner. It is to his innermost being that he speaks, to that part of himself that, ostensibly, stands apart from material concerns and earthly considerations. It is to the part of himself that centers on the eternal that he gives what in retrospect can be seen, with pathos, as only a temporal assurance of comfort and security. His is the ultimate exercise in self-delusion: he has attempted to convince himself that, in the most perishable of possessions, he can find solace and permanence.

The parable's warning — "this night your soul will be required of you" — speaks only to those who believe in an afterlife, and one in which mortals are

12. New Testament scholar Luise Schottroff points out that this parable, like most of Jesus' stories, likely has a Hebraic rather than a Greek background and that its linkage with Epicurean thought is, therefore, doubtful. As is not uncommon in homiletic exercises, I have taken a bit of exegetical license!

13. Dr. Schottroff also points out that the farmer may well have been behaving as a proto-capitalist, building the storage capacity to be able to keep his crops off the market until he could sell at an optimum price.

required to account for their behavior in this existence. Such a warning does not pose a problem for the Epicurean, but, given the choice, I opt for the Christian alternative. Belief that we have to account for ourselves may well be an illusion all of its own but it is, for me, a far more satisfying answer to the irrationalities and inequities of life on this planet.

Support for this view, albeit for very pragmatic social reasons, comes from a curious source. The social biologist Ashley Montagu, while certainly no fan of Christian sentiments, suggests that the idea of immortality has a more immediate significance for the order and stability of modern societies.

> The desire for eternal happiness and the fear of eternal punishment have been among the strongest factors in causing men to adhere to whatever their society conceived to be the good life that we know. And I cannot help but think that with the unready and premature jettisoning of such beliefs in certain parts of the western world there has gone a breakdown in the moral fiber of large numbers of persons who would not otherwise have been left spiritually rudderless in a world at sea.
>
> We know that at the present time millions of men and women live for the moment, and have learned to live for the future only insofar as the moment matters. . . . And this bring me to what I believe is an eternally important truth. It is, that those who have not learned how to die have not learned how to live. This, it would appear, is one of the ends which the belief in immortality is calculated to secure. . . . If one believes one doesn't have to die well, there seems to be no particular point to living well — and by well I mean according to the canons of moral goodness prevailing in one's society. . . .
>
> Under such conditions of belief the postponement of certain immediate gratifications appears unreasonable and otiose. So to believe [in living in the moment] is impossible for anyone who believes in immortality, and if this fact constituted the main claim of that belief to serious consideration, I suggest it would more than justify [its] presence here.[14]

Years ago, I remember seeing the play *Teahouse of the August Moon.* The one line I remember from that drama says something like, "pain makes one think, thinking makes one wise, wisdom makes life endurable." Perhaps this is especially true regarding the pain that is experienced when we lose those who

14. Ashley Montagu, *Immortality* (New York: Grove, 1955), pp. 51, 53.

are nearest and dearest to us. The loss is a pain that is like no other and it does force us to think — about life, about our own mortality, and about the future, both ours and that of the ones we have loved and lost.

It is this contemplation that has produced, for many, what Sir James Frazier once called the "momentous creed" of immortality. Its discussion, Frazier noted,

> can hardly fail to be at once instructive and impressive, whether we regard the record with complacency as a noble testimony to the aspiring genius of man, who claims to outlive the sun and the stars, or whether we view it with pity as a melancholy monument of fruitless labour and barren ingenuity expended in prying into that great mystery of which fools profess their knowledge and wise men confess their ignorance.[15]

It may be that immortality is, as Joseph Addison put it, only a "fond desire" or "a pleasing hope." If so, it is the oldest and most enduring human illusion, for its traces are to be found in the most ancient of recorded civilizations. Some of earth's oldest monuments are, as Frazier observed, testaments to a belief in an afterlife. It is almost as though the existence of the ancient Egyptian pyramids, for example — built not only as tombs but as passageways for the soul to traverse from this world to the next — stand as a permanent rebuke to those who would question or doubt the reality of both realms.

For those who demand incontrovertible proof of immortality — of the sort that only scientific certitude can provide — nothing we have by way of knowledge will suffice. This is the dilemma faced by those whose lives are "planned upon the certainties of this world rather than upon conjectures about a world to come."[16] It is a problem bequeathed to us, in large measure, by a modern age that has solved many of the world's riddles and, in the process, given the impression that all of life's questions are answerable. Ours is an age that has lost much of the sense of mystery that enveloped previous generations. To the extent that mystery rested upon ignorance and superstition, the loss is a gain. But to the degree that this loss of mystery marks the loss of awe, wonder, and hope of the sort that moved the ancients to build pyramids and cathedrals, it is a great loss indeed. It is why, for my small part, the pain that death brings and the reflection on that painful loss — while it may not offer any ironclad assurances — does serve to make this life endurable. It is a pain that leads to the promise of the One who said, "I am the resurrection and the life."

15. Quoted in Montagu, *Immortality*, pp. vii-viii.

16. Hudson, *Truths We Live By*, p. 119.

Chapter 9

A Skeptic's Plea

Mark 9:14-29

In all of Scripture, there is likely no more sympathetic figure than that unnamed and unknown father whose plight is recorded in the Gospel of Mark, who comes and pleads to Jesus to cure his son.[1] The child appears to suffer from epileptic seizures — those, at least, are the symptoms the father describes — but the nature of the illness is unimportant. Mainly, we are drawn in this story to the agony of the father who is desperately seeking help, from any source, that might restore his son to health.

It is significant that this story is told about a man who is not identified in any way. Elsewhere, Mark provides some personal information, albeit brief, regarding the people who seek Jesus' help: The name of the man whose daughter is at the point of death and who beseeches Jesus to make her well is Jairus, a lay leader of the local synagogue (5:22-24; 35-42). The woman whose daughter also seems to be afflicted with epilepsy and whose unwillingness to accept an initial rebuff from Jesus eventually provokes a positive response is identified as a Syrian from the Phoenician coast (7:25-30). It is as if Mark wishes to establish specific identities of those whom Jesus healed so that there could be no dispute about the authenticity of these accounts. Here, however, we have no clue as to the identity of this poor chap. To Mark, he is a face in the crowd that has been drawn to Jesus, either by the excitement surrounding

1. The story of this father can also be found in Matthew 17:14-21 and Luke 9:37-42.

Jesus' acts of healing or the controversy those acts created. Whether this man is wealthy or poor, influential or unknown in the community, well educated or illiterate, we do not know, and it does not seem to matter as far as the story is concerned. We only know that the man is an anguished father, and, in this respect, he comes to us as a representative of every parent who has suffered the agony of having a seriously ill child and who has been fearfully uncertain about the child's recovery.

The Request

Whoever this man might have been, he comes to Jesus with a simple, straightforward request. He beseeches Jesus to "have pity on us and help us." It is a frightfully candid moment, for this father's plea is both for his son and for himself. This is not some noble, self-effacing cry that has only the well-being of the child in mind, nor is it one of those romanticized stories in which the parent does not think of himself but only of his offspring. It is the child who is physically ill but it is the father who is in emotional turmoil and who desperately seeks Jesus' aid, for himself as well as for his son. This father is a man who is in a situation of sheer desperation; nevertheless, he is honest about his own emotions. His son needs help but so does he as well!

The father does not ask that his son be healed, only that Jesus take pity on their plight. In one respect, this may be viewed as quite odd. We may assume that this is no casual encounter between Jesus and this man; in all likelihood, the father had heard of Jesus' growing reputation in the region for being able to work miracles. It can be presumed that he deliberately set out to find Jesus and to ask for his help. We wonder then why the father is not quite specific about what he wishes; why not ask that his son be cured rather than ask Jesus to take pity on the two of them?

In another sense, however, the request is all the more poignant because the father asks only for pity and help, not for a cure. It deepens our understanding of the anguish this man must have felt: he has already asked Jesus' disciples for their assistance and, for some reason, they have been unable to cure the child. It appears to be just after the disciples' failure that Jesus happens on the scene and finds his disciples in the midst of a crowd of scribes and engaged in an intense discussion with them, possibly offering excuses for or seeking to defend their inability to be of any help to the stricken child. It is clear that the father and his child were the topic of conversation because Jesus asks, when the entire throng runs to greet him, what the hubbub is all about. It is then that the father — "one of the crowd," as Mark simply describes him

— answers, and after describing the child's symptoms, says, "Teacher, I brought my son to you because I asked your disciples for help but they were unable to assist us." It is as though this father has grown doubtful about the possibility that his son can be helped and, steeling himself against any further disappointment, does not even ask for a cure.

The Response

For me, at least, it will forever remain a mystery why Jesus says to the father, "Anything is possible to the person who believes." I do not find the commentaries on this passage to be especially helpful regarding Jesus' response.

Most commentators find Jesus' answer consistent with his "utter confidence in God" — the conviction that if one believes enough, all things are possible. This, of course, fits well with the position taken by many of today's spokespersons for God who make God's power conditional on the degree of our faith. Other commentators interpret these words as an expression of astonishment that anyone — in this case, the father — would question the power of God to heal. They see Jesus' response as a rebuke to the father's request: to the father who asks, "If you can do anything, have pity on us and help us," these commentators have Jesus answering, in effect, "What do you mean 'if'? The problem is not what God can do but how much you believe in God's power to do any and every thing."

Under either circumstance, Jesus' response, though many may find it religiously correct, has a harshness that seems to me to border on cruelty. Why, I find myself asking, would Jesus make the cure of the child conditional on his father's faith? Even if one grants the position of the traditionalists that this story is all about the power of faith, why should it not be the child's faith that is at issue? It is the son who is ill, so should it not be the son's — not the father's — trust in Jesus' healing abilities that is paramount?

Of course, all sorts of reasons may be offered for why the child does not speak for himself. Perhaps he is too young; perhaps the seizures render him incapable of expressing himself. It is possible the child has no sense whatsoever of what is taking place; he might have no idea what faith and trust mean. Or perhaps Jesus senses the father's lack of faith and is putting him to a test. But the question persists: why should the child's cure depend on the father's faith?

If we knew no more of the story than this, we might ask what would have happened if the father had replied differently. Suppose the father had replied, "I'm sorry, Jesus. I would like to have faith in God and in your power to help but I've had too many disappointments and my son has suffered too many setbacks. Even your own disciples have been of no help whatsoever to me and my son. If you can help us, please do so, but don't ask me to believe in miracles when I have experienced nothing but dashed hopes." If the father failed to display the requisite amount of faith, would Jesus have failed to help the child? If so, then the child is only a helpless pawn in a larger drama of faith and trust being played out between Jesus and the child's parent. This surely is not the kind of person Jesus is, and it surely wouldn't speak well of the idea of faith and confidence in God — which leads one to wonder whether Jesus is, in fact, actually quite incidental to the whole situation. Is it the father's faith in God that matters and is Jesus then only the messenger, the instrument, of God's healing power? If so, if this story is really about the father's relationship with God, why should the health of the child be totally dependent on circumstances between his father and God, circumstances over which the child has absolutely no control?

If these seem irrelevant or, even worse, irreverent questions, imagine taking one's seriously ill child to a physician and describing the symptoms of the illness only to have the physician say that the cure has nothing to do with any therapy for the child but instead depends on the parent's attitude. I, for one, would not want my child's recovery to turn on the strength of my own sentiments or convictions. I could, of course, tell the physician whatever I think he wants to hear, even if I don't really believe it, and run the risk that the physician would discover what is truly in my heart. But I think I would resent being placed in such a predicament. Most of all, I would be somewhat put off by the pronouncement that my child's health depended on the correctness of my attitude.

Finally, it also remains a mystery as to what the father is supposed to believe in. Is it faith in God that he is expected to express or does Jesus want some acknowledgment and affirmation of his own healing power before he displays it? Is the act of faith in itself an integral part of the healing process? Why, we ask almost in exasperation, does one have to believe at all? If Jesus is the Great Physician who possesses these miraculous abilities, why does he not simply get on with it and use them whenever and wherever he can?

The Plea

We come then to the father's reply to Jesus, which may be the most important part of the entire story. After Jesus states, either as an admonition or as a rebuke, "If you can! All things are possible to him who believes," the father responds, "Lord, I believe; help my unbelief!" Or as Edgar Goodspeed translates this passage, "help my want of faith."

There cannot possibly be a more honest moment in all of recorded religious history than this. Here is a man in despair over that which would bring any parent to the emotional brink. His child apparently suffers from epilepsy, but in the ancient world the child would be presumed to be possessed by an evil spirit. Two thousand years later, most people do not believe in demon possession, but epilepsy remains an illness for which modern medicine has found no cure; it can only be managed with drug therapy. We can only imagine the anguish this malady would have caused a parent two millennia ago, when, in addition to the uncontrollable outbursts the illness spawned, the parent had to contend with the popular assumption that his child was possessed by the Devil.

It is possible to imagine that this father had sought help from every conceivable source he could find. In the ancient world, those sources would have been few; diagnosing an illness as possession by an evil spirit would have quickly removed it from the realm of known medical therapies and consigned it to the world of superstition and magic. It is no wonder, then, that the father seeks help from one who has a reputation as a miracle-worker. The father seeks Jesus as likely his last and only resort.

It is possible also to imagine this father churning in his mind what he would say if he managed to get an audience with Jesus. What would he do to get Jesus' attention? What might he say or do that would call attention to his son's case as somehow warranting attention before or apart from all the other stricken people who were seeking Jesus' help? Could he offer money? Might he pledge his loyalty as a disciple? Was there some other recompense or expression of gratitude that he could extend? The story records none of these considerations or responses. Instead, it simply recounts that this unknown face in the throng, when Jesus asks what the crowd's discussion is all about, states his case succinctly and ends with the plea, "have pity on us."

We have examined Jesus' response and its seeming harshness, making his help conditional on the father's faith. The meaning and significance of that response I leave to those who purport to understand such matters better than I. What transfixes me is the father's reply. The honesty of this man is stunning! He is asked to believe and could have easily proclaimed his faith in Jesus or God or whomever he is expected to trust. How simple it would have been to say, "yes, Lord, I believe," and to have kept his reservations to himself. Why, instead, does he choose to acknowledge his uncertainty about his own convictions?

Rather than conceal his doubts, the father admits them — not boastfully or cynically but as a cry of desperation. We do not sense in the narrative that this man is trying to make a point as to how independent-minded he is or trying to prove that he is not someone who, in a weak moment, would profess a level of belief he does not possess. There is no indication here that we are dealing with anything more or less than a father whose wish, first and foremost, is for the health and well-being of his son but who, at the same time, is not willing to be untruthful about his own inner thoughts. What we have here, therefore, is the biblical example of the skeptic, a man whose convictions do not rise to the level that the circumstances suggest he should display. The man in this story is one who has every reason to be less than straightforward about his beliefs but who admits his doubts even if, by doing so, he risks his son's cure. Surely, there is no greater honesty than this — to admit a lack of faith when faith is the apparent key to the resolution of one's travails!

Commentary

It is not surprising that the crisis moments in our lives present us with the occasions for faith. The illness of a child, the loss of one's job, a relationship that goes sour, a marriage that shows signs of crumbling, the death of a loved one — any unexpected and dismaying event will turn many toward the wellsprings of faith. We may feel abandoned by health, material security, or people on whom we depend, but we cast our eyes heavenward, we utter a silent or audible prayer, or we seek solace and reassurance by reading a comforting passage of Scripture. In situations such as these when we find ourselves without the supports on which we routinely depend — when the normal patterns of family, work, leisure, or relationships are suddenly upended by that which is not only unanticipated but also dreaded as a possibility — we are apt to turn to our religious resources, whatever they may be, for aid. Roman Catholics light candles or say the rosary, Protestants fall to their knees; each responds according to the rituals known best in the hope that the moment of crisis will pass and life will return to its regular rhythms.

In moments of crisis, we are apt to believe that the intensity of our faith is a critical ingredient if there is to be a good outcome to whatever it is that we confront. This is certainly the view that every televangelist who promotes faith as essential for healing would have us believe. We are made to feel that crisis moments in our lives are occasions on which the slightest amount of doubt would be not only inappropriate but perilous. Consequently, in moments of crisis we are our most devout selves; we are wont to "cast all our cares," as the Scriptures prescribe, on the One who cares for us.

Nevertheless, crisis moments are not only occasions of faith but moments of skepticism and doubt, be they of slight or of great proportion. When a job is lost we may be anxious, wondering whether we will find new employment, whether this will mean a cut in pay, whether it will require uprooting the family and moving to a new location, or whether the savings will last and unemployment benefits hold out. If the months drag on and the job search is unsuccessful, our skepticism may deepen regarding the future. If we have suffered a severed relationship, we may come to be skeptical of all that preceded the break; we wonder if we were engaged in a huge deception. We can even come to doubt ourselves and our ability to sustain long-term ties. If we are enduring a serious illness, we immediately wonder about the possibility of recovery or a cure. The physician can offer some reassurance but never a guarantee, and that inevitably leaves room for uncertainty. If the prognosis is not hopeful, our uncertainty is heightened and we are inclined to be doubtful about what lies ahead. We may seek second or third opinions, turn to alternative medicines and therapies, cling to every story we hear about a similar case that was cured, or hope in desperation that a new drug will offer aid. And throughout all of our worry, we are likely to find ourselves in the depths of despair as we are tossed between doubt and hope.

Such must have been the turmoil of the father of the epileptic child — within the drastically limited options available two thousand years ago. He comes to Jesus in the hope that the Lord will cure his afflicted son, but when he is asked if he has faith, he confesses that he lacks it. There is some part of the process about which the father has honest doubts. He is a skeptic, he admits his skepticism, and his response to Jesus is the skeptic's plea: Lord, I believe; help me in spite of my inadequate faith.

The remarkable climax to this extraordinary story is that, in the end, the cure of the son is not made to turn on the father's degree of faith. The quantity, depth, or quality of the father's trust proves, in the end, to have no bearing on Jesus' willingness to restore his son to health. Having listened to this man acknowledge his lack of faith, Jesus nevertheless proceeds to heal the child. It is as if Jesus wished to have the father consider the importance of hope and confidence in the midst of his desperate situation but, once the father has done so, he answers his plea without condition or reservation.

Christianity might have a much greater appeal in the modern world if its purveyors took this story of skepticism more seriously. The incessant demands that Jesus be personally accepted before any of his saving power can be claimed or the insistence that unwavering faith is the sine qua non of Christian living — both so prevalent today — leave out of their purview countless biblical examples of redemptive encounters between Jesus and the people whose paths he crossed, many of whom did not accept him as their personal Savior or believe unreservedly in his mission and message. Many of the Gospel accounts, in fact, are stories of people who were not quite certain about this itinerant teacher from Galilee — an uncertainty that begins with his own family. That many of these individuals became disciples later does not obscure the fact that they began their journey with Jesus as uncertain associates — questioning, wondering, expressing bafflement and misgivings.

The faith of those who were companions of Jesus is the more compelling, to a considerable degree, because it was not an automatic, unreflective response on their part to the Master and his message. Many of his first disciples greeted Jesus in the way that we would be inclined to greet anyone today who announced that he or she was sent from God and possessed miraculous powers. They were skeptical — Jesus, after all, was not the only person in the precincts of ancient Palestine who made such seemingly extravagant claims. And the Bible seems perfectly comfortable with their skepticism. In fact, we can only assume that stories such as that of this skeptical father are recorded in Scripture because its authors and its Author wish us to know that skepticism is quite permissible in the eye of God.

Skepticism is not for the faint of heart. The skeptic's journey is not nearly as comfortable and constantly reassuring as is that of the believer who never finds occasion for question or doubt. It also can be a healthy corrective for many of those who are on what are today's paths of religious correctness — "faith journeys," which at times can appear to be any spiritual quest in which the journeyers are unsure of where it is they wish to go. The skeptic's journey forces the pilgrim to stop and reflect on the path he or she trods, rather than flitting from one ecstatic experience to the next.

Skepticism is the sentiment to which we turn when faith falters. The father in this story admits his lack of faith; his skepticism lies in whatever doubt he harbors about whether his son can, in fact, be cured. His words are *help me, where my faith fails!* It may sounds too much like agnosticism or something worse for us to utter this same plea, in spite of the fact that we confront countless situations in which our faith — in other persons and things on whom we depend — also fails us. The stock market fails to live up to the expectations — the faith, if you will — that many people place in it, as though its rise is inevitable and one's wealth therefrom is guaranteed. The belief of many couples in the permanence of their marriage, of parents in the success of their children, of workers in the security of their jobs are all experiences in life where that on which we trust and depend sometimes lets us down. In such moments we become skeptics because we become doubters — not only about other people and things but about ourselves, our choices, and our abilities.

If, in such moments, our doubts cause us to question ourselves, to reexamine our lives and our priorities, and to search for ways in which we can better our condition, then our skepticism will have served us well. We must be careful not to make skepticism into a philosophy of life, but we should be equally hesitant to turn it into a vice. The counsel of Josiah Royce, noted near the beginning of this book, is both wise and timely: "doubt is never the proper end of thinking, but it is a good beginning."

Chapter 10

Groping for God

> *From one ancestor he made all nations to inhabit the whole earth . . . so that they would search for God and perhaps grope for him and find him, though indeed he is not far from each one of us.*
>
> Acts 17:26-27, New Revised Standard Version

According to orthodox Christian teaching, humankind would know nothing about God were it not for God's revelation, first to the Israelites at Mount Sinai through the Law and then to the world through the life, death, and resurrection of Jesus of Nazareth. Knowledge of God comes, then, not from contemplating the realm of nature and the orderly cycles of the universe from which one might deduce the activity of a divine creator, but from the Word given initially to the chosen of God at Mount Sinai in a set of divine precepts and commandments, and finally in the Word that was made flesh and dwelt among the men and women of ancient Palestine, the Word whose message has been preserved for all times in the writings of sacred Scripture, and whose spirit resides in the hearts of all true believers.

It is impossible, according to the orthodox view, for humans to "find God" by exerting any human effort or ingenuity. In the famous language of Karl Barth, one of orthodoxy's most renowned defenders, since God is "wholly other" than anything the mind of mortals can conceive, any attempt from a human perspective to apprehend God is doomed — as a display of human pride and arrogance — to failure. Christian orthodoxy echoes the sentiments of the prophet Isaiah:

> For my thoughts are not your thoughts,
> neither are your ways my ways, says the LORD.

For as the heavens are higher than the earth,
so are my ways higher than your ways
and my thoughts than your thoughts. (55:8-9)

There is much to be said for this orthodox view regarding the possibility of knowledge of God. Its major achievement is to save us from the arrogance of making God a projection of what we humans imagine ourselves to be when we are at our best. This temptation to think of God in human terms is ever with us. It manifests itself in relatively innocent, if innocuous, ways in Sunday school depictions of the Almighty and in all the anthropomorphic language we use in efforts to describe God as thinking, acting, and feeling in the same way we mortals do. We are constantly subject to the risk of thinking of God as a superhuman being. Against this temptation, the view of Christian orthodoxy says that God is above and beyond human imagining and that we can know nothing of God except for the fact that God chooses to be revealed to us.

Obviously, from the orthodox perspective, the idea of humans searching for God is quite an improper — indeed, fundamentally impossible — undertaking. And yet this is precisely what Paul appears to applaud the philosophers he encountered on Mars Hill in Athens for doing! According to the account in the Acts of the Apostles, the philosophers had heard Paul preaching about Jesus and the resurrection and they wished to know more "about this new doctrine" that Paul propounded, one that introduced "new ideas that sound strange." It is to these philosophers that Paul said, "I see that in everything that concerns religion you are uncommonly scrupulous." He then proceeded to proclaim the God "you worship but do not know," who, Paul declared, has created "all nations to inhabit the whole earth," so that they would "search for God and perhaps grope for him and find him."[1]

It is almost New Age language that Paul uses as he describes both the divine scheme and the human quest. Certainly it is not the language of orthodoxy! To "search," "grope," "seek," "touch," and "find" all suggest a very human process of exploration and discovery. In fact, it sounds all too human — almost as if a sightless person was engaged in the attempt to identify an object and could only approach it by groping, touching, and feeling. Clearly, Paul envisions here a process that is initiated by human will and that reaches up

1. It is a pity that the notion of groping has come to have such a negative connotation in the modern vocabulary, suggesting the activity of perverts rather than the quest of earnest seekers after God. Such is the debasement not only of language in our age but also of the human imagination, in which the sensation of touch and the idea of passionate discovery are reduced to matters of sex. Groping for God is a passion of a different order!

and out in the effort to discover God; it is not God revealed to humankind that Paul describes but humankind in search of, and finding, God.

It may well be, of course, that Paul has chosen to adopt language and thought-forms that would appeal to the particular group of listeners he was addressing on this occasion. We know, from other references, that Paul was quite adept at this technique of communication. But it is impossible to escape the realization that, if this is what Paul is doing, he does so at the expense of a major premise of orthodox Christian belief, i.e., that mortals might search for but they cannot find God. Here, Paul says seeking God is not only possible but commendable!

In this incident, we encounter once again — or rather Paul did — the Epicureans, whose desire for an existence unburdened by pain and devoted to securing the maximum amount of pleasure in life we noted earlier. On Mars Hill where Paul spoke, the Epicureans were in the company of Stoics, members of a second major school of Greek philosophy. Together, these two schools represented the principal Greek philosophical viewpoints of the day. Unlike the Epicureans, however, Stoic philosophy was not oriented toward ideas of pleasure-seeking. The Stoics taught that duty, rather than pleasure, is life's chief aim — duty not "in some grandiose and vast blank categorical imperative, but duty in the smaller relations of life, to one's friends, to one's tasks, to one's neighbor, to oneself."[2]

Also unlike the Epicureans who, as we have seen, were disdainful of the idea of immortality, the Stoics were of two minds regarding the subject. One faction suggested that the souls of mortals have a continued existence after death while another thought immortality was attainable only by the wise. Seneca (4 B.C.–A.D. 65), a leading Roman Stoic who would have been a contemporary of Jesus and Paul, was a principal exponent of the first view; he discoursed at some length on the happiness or misery of the soul after death. This difference between the Stoics and the Epicureans is likely reflected in the account in Acts, which states that after Paul mentioned the subject of the resurrection, "some [probably the Epicureans] scoffed; and others [likely Stoics] said, 'we will hear you on this subject some other time'" (17:32).

To UNDERSTAND THIS PASSAGE it may be useful to look at the original Greek text. What we find is that Paul has used two different Greek verbs to describe the activity that "the nations" — which God created from a common source — will pursue in their quest for God. The first verb is one that is incredibly

2. Irwin Edman, introduction to *Epictetus* (Roslyn, N.Y.: Walter J. Black, 1944), pp. xiii-xiv.

rich, with all sorts of interpretative possibilities; it appears throughout the New Testament in a number of intriguing contexts. It is the word which translates "search" or "seek"; in the Mars Hill address, the verb appears in the phrase, "that they would search after God" (NERV), which is also translated as "that they should seek the Lord" (KJV) or "seek God" (RSV). Here the usage is similar to that in Matthew's Gospel in which this verb appears in the parable of the shepherd who loses one of his sheep and leaves his flock to go and seek or search for the one sheep that has strayed (18:12). The same idea of searching is found in the parable of the merchant "searching for fine pearls," of whom Jesus says, "this is a picture of the kingdom of heaven" (13:45). Similarly in the Gospel of Luke, there is the story of Mary and Joseph, who, on returning from a family trip to Jerusalem, find Jesus missing and return to the city where they find him in the temple. Mary says, "Your father and I have been searching for you" (2:48-49).

Matthew's Gospel also uses this same verb when telling the story of Judas, who, from the moment he received the thirty pieces of silver, "sought" or "looked out for an opportunity" to betray Jesus (26:16). And Matthew uses the same verb in the account of Jesus' Sermon on the Mount: "seek first" or "strive for" the kingdom of God (or as the New English Bible translates this statement, "set your mind on . . ."). Mark, on the other hand, uses this verb in yet another sense when he says, "the chief priests and doctors of the law *deliberated* regarding some way of making away with Jesus" (11:18, my italics).

Both Paul and Peter like to use this verb in the sense of "to pursue," as in Paul's letter to the Romans — "to those who pursue glory, honor and immortality, he will give eternal life" (2:7) — and Peter's admonition that "whoever loves life . . . must . . . seek peace and pursue it" (1 Peter 3:10-11). All these variations in meaning of the first verb that Paul uses in his speech in Athens suggest what he might have wished to convey by stating that humankind should search after God.

If we look at the use of this same verb from a slightly different perspective — as it appears in Greek literary and philosophical circles — two interesting, additional translations appear. Diogenes Laertius, the second-century (A.D.) Greek writer, uses the verb to mean "ask for." But Plato, the quintessential Greek philosopher, uses the verb to mean "inquire into" or "examine," as in philosophical investigations. This brings us closer to what the philosophers in Paul's audience might have understood him to mean or imply.

Unlike the verb usually translated as "to search" or "to seek," the second verb Paul uses is a rarity in Scripture. It can mean "to touch," as in Jesus' invitation to his disciples after his resurrection to "touch me and see" (Luke 24:39). It can also mean "to grope for" or "grope after," as it does here in Paul's

Athens address. Here again, the Greek verb appears throughout Greek literature; it is found in the *Odyssey* of Homer, in Plato, and in the writings of the historian Polybius. As with the philosophical meaning of "search" (i.e., to inquire into or examine), Paul's audience would have been quite familiar with his use of the term "to grasp after." Is it possible, perhaps, that Paul chose this verb with a deliberate double meaning — anticipating that the philosophers in his Mars Hill audience would think of seeking for God as a philosophical exercise, while at the same time implying that the one who truly seeks the Infinite must do so not by philosophical deliberations but by groping, as if blind, in order to "feel and touch" the face of God?

Under any of the foregoing possibilities, it seems the search for God is very much a spiritually legitimate human endeavor. Whether and wherever one is looking for an opportunity to encounter God, or pursuing, asking for, deliberating about, inquiring into, or groping after things divine, Paul assures his hearers and his readers that such effort can be rewarded and that God is not "far from each of us."

THE IMAGERY OF GROPING or grasping after inclines one to think of persons in a confused state — perhaps in a dark and unfamiliar corridor — reaching out hesitantly, half in hope of finding something solid or familiar to hold onto and half in fear of touching something harmful or possibly even repulsive. We grope when we are not sure of where we are going. Even when we are certain what we seek — perhaps something we have mislaid — "groping" suggests that we are not quite certain how or where to look for it.

Are these appropriate images or visions of the effort to find God? Certainly they are not for the person who demands an absolutely clear, straight, untroubled path to the Infinite. But clearly Paul thought that "groping" was an appropriate description of the search for God, or at least appropriate on this occasion. And yet, in this image Paul suggests a process that is neither rational nor logical. That would seem strange in a discussion with Greek philosophers, for above all else, ancient philosophy valued the rational mind. For Aristotle, the "exercise of [one's] vital faculties on one side in obedience to reason and on the other side with reason" is humans' principal function, and that which sets us apart from plants, animals, and any other forms of life.

> [S]urely as [our] several members, eye and hand and foot, plainly have each [their] own function, so we must suppose that [humans have] some function over and above all these. What then is it? . . . [The human] function then being, as we say, a kind of life — that is to say, ex-

> ercise of one's faculties and action of various kinds with reason — the good [person's] function is to do this well or nobly.[3]

Logic is the essential tool of the philosopher, so much so, in fact, that Bertrand Russell once pronounced that "all philosophy is logic." Logic is used by philosophy to examine the ways in which truth is attained, verified, and interpreted; it is possibly one of the reasons the Epicureans found the idea of a resurrection so incomprehensible. If, therefore, Paul is attempting to speak to the philosophers on Mars Hill in terms that they would readily understand — "in their own language," so to speak — why would he use an image that would possibly offend their basic philosophical instincts?

We have to recognize that what the Book of the Acts records is, in all likelihood, only a digest or summary of what Paul said, and that therefore we do not have the full text of his address. It is also possible that what has been recorded are Paul's introductory remarks; if so, he may have gone on to make a far more amplified case for the Christian message. But we must deal with what we have, and what we have suggests that Paul, in addition to invoking an approach to God that does not rely on reason and logic, also sought to disabuse his audience of the idea that God could be represented in human form or found in shrines such as those that would have surrounded Paul and his audience at every turn.

What Paul seems to do initially in this address is to describe a search for the Divine that, on one hand, appeals to the best intellectual instincts of the philosophers in his audience and, on the other, is radically different from that which these same philosophers would have endorsed. The search he describes is also, however, one that departs from what the orthodox among his modern Christian counterparts would approve. It is, in fact, a quest that begins with human initiative, and that initiative, Paul suggests, is the first step on the road to finding God.

It may be at this point that Paul had in mind his own journey of faith and discovery. He must have reflected frequently on his early career as a devout Jew who was so convinced the followers of Jesus were dangerous heretics that he undertook the mission of having them arrested and thrown in jail. Perhaps he saw himself, in retrospect, as groping for God during this period in his life, in spite of the fact that he had been pursuing what was, to him, a reasonable, logical course and cause — that of suppressing religious heresy. If not during this stage in his life, this imagery must have been especially strong in his mind

3. Quoted in Robert Black, *Perspectives in Philosophy* (New York: Holt, Rinehart and Winston, 1961), pp. 55-56.

when he recalled his experience on the road to Damascus. It was there that he was literally blinded and his companions had to lead him by the hand to the city.

Imagine Paul during those three days in Damascus, sightless and fasting! Unable to be distracted by his physical surroundings, he had only his thoughts to occupy his mind. Did he ponder where he had gone wrong, or wonder if his vision of the One whose followers he persecuted was an illusion? Was he overwhelmed with guilt and remorse at the thought of having hounded innocent people, or suddenly in a state of immense confusion about his own convictions?

Scripture tells us nothing of what Paul did or thought for those three days, except that he did not take food or drink. It must have been, for Paul, three days of agony as he searched for answers to what, at that moment, was the most startling experience of his life. It might be argued that the answer to Paul's predicament was clear since Jesus had revealed himself to Paul on the Damascus road. Even granting this, however, Paul was still left in a state of uncertainty for three days, not knowing what to do or what would be asked of him.

What Paul pointed to, in his speech to the philosophers at Athens, was therefore likely a description of his own quest for God — one in which he was certain he had all the answers until he was radically brought to the realization that his answers fell short of God's question to him. Good Pharisee that he was, well-versed in the Hebrew Scriptures, he may well have remembered the passage in the Book of Deuteronomy — "The LORD will smite you with madness and blindness and confusion of mind; and you shall grope at noonday, as the blind grope in darkness" (28:28-29) — as an apt description of his Damascus-road experience and its three-day aftermath. Or he may have recalled the pronouncements of Job: "[God] takes the wise in their own craftiness; and the schemes of the wily are brought to a quick end. They meet with darkness in the daytime, and grope at noonday as in the night" (5:13-14). He may also have thought of Isaiah's lament: "We look for light, and behold, darkness, and for brightness, but we walk in gloom. We grope for the wall like the blind; we grope like those who have no eyes; we stumble at noon as in the twilight" (59:9-10).

The idea of groping for God is undoubtedly one that had personal meaning and significance for Paul. It is not surprising that he chose to make it a part of his message to the crowd in Athens, for whom he must have felt both an intellectual and spiritual kinship. Two thousand years later, it is an idea and an image that appeals to many for whom the Divine does not come neatly packaged and presented, as many contemporary electronic marketers of God would have it, but instead is grasped and found only after long, earnest nights of the soul in which one gropes for the Light which is eternal and everlasting.

IN 1951, PAUL TILLICH GAVE the James W. Richard Lectures at the University of Virginia; the lectures were subsequently published under the title *Biblical Religion and the Search for Ultimate Reality.* The title reflects Tillich's lifelong quest as well as the immense contribution he made to modern theological thought — his own searching for God and his passionate insistence on making use of the tools of philosophical inquiry and well as theological analysis in the search for answers to the Divine Mystery.

In this brief work and with the intellectual rigor and precision that made him one of the twentieth century's preeminent theologians, Tillich explores some of the same questions that have occupied us in this chapter. "Religion," he declares, "is a function of the human mind"; for this reason, he notes, it represents for many theologians "the futile attempt of man to reach God. Religion moves from man toward God, while revelation moves from God to man, and its first work is to confound man's religious aspirations."[4] If the Bible constitutes the record of God's self-disclosure to humankind then how is it possible, Tillich asks in a self-critique of his own title, to speak of "biblical religion"?

Tillich's answer provides an added insight into Paul's notion of groping for God. To those who reject this idea — those for whom religion and philosophy "are attempts of man to be like God . . . demonic elevations of man above his creatureliness and finitude" — Tillich points out that revelation "must be received and that the name for the reception of revelation is religion."[5] Here, then, is a humble but profound reminder that we are not hapless pawns in some divine game of chess. God reaches toward those who have been created in the divine image and likeness; God seeks the one element of creation that has the capacity to reply "yes" or "no" to the Divine's gracious goodness.

Our human searching, therefore, occurs because we alone, as far as we know — of all God's creation — enjoy the freedom to accept or reject the divine impulse. We grope precisely because we are not automatons. We do not have to respond in some preordained manner to God's prescription for our

4. Paul Tillich, *Biblical Religion and the Search for Ultimate Reality* (Chicago: University of Chicago Press, 1955), p. 2.

5. Tillich, *Biblical Religion,* pp. 2-3.

lives. We grope because we can be and are lured by other attractions and alternative possibilities; it is our felt and very human need to explore and examine our other options that makes us weigh the sacred alternative in our living against all the alluring, secular options that array themselves constantly before us.

In the technology-enriched comfort of the twenty-first century, the secular options are immense. It is possible to live one's life completely shut off and isolated from the world's pain and misery. We can surround ourselves with cell phones, digital television, and laptops, spending our days in a mechanistic environment that has no place for suffering or distress. We can commute to our jobs and back home again on the depressed ditches we call freeways that free us from having, as we once did, to drive through the city's wretched areas. Without ever leaving our computer, we can shop and browse, plan vacations and sell stocks; where once we asked gas station attendants for directions and sales clerks for assistance, the Internet now provides us with door-to-door travel details and the opportunity to make our purchases without any personal encounters. In this modern way, we can complete a myriad of chores that once obliged us to interact with and experience other humans who do not enjoy our advantages. For many, ours is truly a "virtual reality" — a world in which, with the multiple gadgets that a technological universe affords, we can shut ourselves off from the realities of life as it is lived by seven-eighths of the world's populace.

Paul's admonition, that we grope for a God who is not very far from us, is both an assurance and a warning. On one hand, it gives us hope and an incentive to reach for the highest that human aspiration and effort can envision. But on the other hand, it serves to remind us how easy it is to become impressed by and enmeshed in the lesser possibilities and thereby to miss what God calls us to be.

A final note: searching for God is not an intellectual exercise in which one explores — at leisure and without any commitment to the outcome of one's quest — the options for conducting one's life. The person who gropes for God has already determined that the object being sought is worthy of all one's striving. One gropes for God almost in desperation — certainly in the realization that to grasp anything less is to take hold of that which will not endure. Groping for God is what we find we must do, after we have discovered that nothing else in this world is worth the effort.

Epilogue

One of the classic works of Holocaust literature is Jean-François Steiner's *Treblinka*. It is a narrative of the death camp located fifty miles from Warsaw that was the major center for the liquidation of Warsaw's Jewish populace. In less than thirteen months — from July 1942, when the first trainload of victims arrived until August 2, 1943, when the camp was destroyed in an extraordinary uprising — 800,000 people perished in Treblinka's gas chambers.

Early in the narrative, an exchange takes place between two camp inmates. Steiner describes one of them, Max Berliner, as a Polish Jew who as a young man had gone to Argentina, where he made his fortune; Berliner returns to Warsaw at the outbreak of the war in a vain attempt to persuade his parents to return with him to Argentina, and he is caught in the general roundup of Warsaw Jews and deported to Treblinka. The other, Pinhas Alter, is a member of the Hasidim whose entire family has been gassed upon arrival in the camp. Berliner is persuaded that the death camp is proof that a God who created the world has failed in his work. Alter is convinced that the ordeal of Treblinka must somehow be understood as the will of God. Steiner describes Pinhas Alter as a fanatic and, as such, beyond the reach of human emotion; so dedicated is he to obeying God's will that nothing touches him. Berliner, on the other hand, is a man who, because the death camp experience has led him to the depths of despair, suffers as only a human being can suffer.

In Pinhas Alter and Max Berliner, Steiner has captured the modern predicament. Berliner and Alter represent two irreconcilable positions prevalent in our time. On one hand, there are those for whom everything that happens in life is the unfolding of a divine plan or part and parcel of God's unfathomable will and purpose. Others, however, are persuaded that a God whose will encompasses the death of children in gas chambers is a God unworthy of worship. Somewhere between these two polarities, those who grope for God seek meaning and understanding.

Many people, like Pinhas Alter, maintain the belief that whatever happens in life and this world is God's will. To depict them as fanatics is too harsh a judgment, as this is as often the faith of the pious as it is that of the pompous. It is difficult, nevertheless, to know just how to respond to people who make this claim. It is not uncommon for well-meaning persons to utter such pronouncements to parents who lose their child to some dread disease, to a grief-stricken person who mourns the loss of a loved one in a freak or sudden accident, or to someone in the midst of some other mind-numbing calamity.

Declaring that pain and suffering, on the one hand, or human evil, on the other, is the will of God either makes of God a demonic figure or else provides an excuse for the malevolence of mortals. Such pronouncements, to many ears, are either in the worst of taste or blasphemous. If the will-of-God assertion has any meaning at all, it can never be offered to others as an explanation for why some otherwise inexplicably tragic occurrence has taken place. It can only be meaningful for the one who makes it as a commentary on an event in his or her own life, and even here one wishes such a person had a better sense of the divine.

Max Berliner's plight is equally problematic. He is, in Steiner's description, a man without God and without hope. He finds himself unable to believe in a God who permits such an atrocity as the Holocaust to occur, but this leaves him with nothing left to believe in except himself and, in the end, he becomes consumed by only one thought — that of revenge.

If these are our only two alternatives — belief in a God whose will we cannot understand and sometimes find inexplicably cruel or belief in ourselves — we are in miserable circumstances. That is why, faced with two possibilities, we search for a third — and that third possibility is likely to be found in searching for meaning in the midst of moments in our lives, such as times of personal suffering, and moments in history, such as the Holocaust, that appear to be devoid of meaning and filled only with dread.

In his letter to the Christians at Ephesus, Paul acknowledged half of the modern plight. He wrote that, as Gentiles, the Ephesians were once without God and without hope (Ephesians 2:12). But Paul did not have to contend with the reality of the Holocaust, with the agonizing questions about God that arise in the aftermath of the slaughter of his covenanted people. There are Jews who solemnly contend that the Holocaust occurred because the Jewish people broke the covenant, and there are Christians who piously proclaim that God has established a new and better covenant that supercedes that made with the people of Israel. Neither view provides an answer for those who ask about the trustworthiness of a God who not only punishes covenant breakers and breaks one covenant in favor of another, but who also would either send or allow infants and children to go to the gas chambers in the name of a broken or a changed compact.

But who are we to ask or demand that God be trustworthy? We need neither ask nor demand; it is God who is presented to us in the long stream of biblical history as One who is worthy of our trust. If the Holocaust has given us reason to raise new questions about that claim and if the seeming intractableness of racial bigotry in modern life also seems to belie that assertion, what recourse do we have?

We end where we began, or at least I return to the point at which I began this journey. I am left with questions about God, to be sure, but my truly great misgivings are about God's creation — about the men and women on this earth who, either in God's name or in denial of God, have shown the world the face of evil. The hard evidence for the proposition that justice and peace are the ends of the human struggle and that life extends beyond this earthly realm may be faint, but the record of human malevolence is overwhelming and irrefutable. If it is a question of trustworthiness, we mortals are much more a question mark than God!

In the end, groping for God amid the debris of death, the deaths of the six million, and the detritus of racial thinking is not simply an act of faith — it is an act of defiance. It requires one to go against all the accumulated evidence that stands as a denial of anything that might be considered divine and eternal — the evidence of the casket in the grave, of a mountain of corpses, or of deadening acts of bigotry. It demands resisting the temptation to believe that these earthbound realities represent truths about life and the world. It necessitates a scornful rejection of those who would have humankind live life under their influence. Groping for God is to search for answers and convictions that affirm a better reality as the truth about life and the human condition.

To deny that the world's frequent eruptions of madness define the nature and character of human existence takes a considerable amount of courage. Not only is the human record replete with acts of individual and collective horror, what is worse, this record seems to continue unabated. Where there are not actual outbursts of collective violence, world leaders persist in their preoccupation with either anticipating mayhem or proposing it, and with the expenditure of immense sums to advance its possibility or ostensibly protect against its occurrence. As if incidents of individual mayhem do not sufficiently abound, the electronic media devote entire telecasts to programs that display interpersonal conflict and violence, while recording industries spend millions promoting the music of alleged artists whose skill consists in displays of verbal violence — defaming women and exalting brutality. A preoccupation with the actual or potential fruits of human aggression in all of its many forms — from domestic abuse to the violence that is war and genocide — continues to be one of the principal hallmarks of our time.

It is in the midst of this relentless avalanche of decay and destruction that one must search for wholeness and inner peace. One searches amidst the decay of a society so devoted to the idol of free enterprise and the acquisition of wealth that it permits the glorification of violence as entertainment and promotes the image of financial success — however it might be obtained — as the highest human achievement. One searches through the brutality that was expressed savagely in the Holocaust and that continues to manifest itself in the thoughtless racial asides of countless persons who are the current equivalent of what the Germans called "parlor Nazis" (individuals who considered the Nazis street thugs but felt they were "right about the Jews"). To search for God, in the face of these threats to social order and human decency, is to affirm that good and not evil is the order of the universe and the code of life. It is a quest for sanity and meaning in the midst of events and conditions that offer up possibilities only for disillusion and despair.

I marvel, as I think back over my life and reflect on the three principal threats to my faith in God — the death of my parents, racism, and the deaths of the six million — that I have never been drawn toward despair. Anger, yes — and, on occasion, dismay over events or circumstances that have highlighted either the absurdity of race as a category of human perception or the unalloyed evil that was the deliberate murder of some six million humans. But neither the reality of race nor that of the Holocaust, nor my grief over the deaths of my parents, has reduced me to despair, to that which Paul Tillich terms "the anxiety of emptiness and meaninglessness."[1]

The alternative to despair is not blind faith. It is, rather, a faith that has faced its doubts and overcome them and that perseveres in spite of all the reasons to abandon the struggle for a better world. This is the powerful message of that unknown author of the Epistle to the Hebrews who asks what faith is: "Faith gives substance to our hopes, and makes us certain of realities we do not see" (11:1).

The writer of the Hebrews epistle proceeds to recite a roll call of saints who lived and died in faith. They include kings, prophets, and a prostitute(!) — all mortals who, the writer says, "overthrew kingdoms, established justice, and saw God's promises fulfilled" (11:33). "These witnesses are around us like a cloud"; should this not be enough to sustain us on our life journeys?

1. Paul Tillich, *The Courage To Be* (New Haven: Yale University Press, 1952), p. 46.

It may not suffice to resolve the harshest questions we face along life's path, but the lives of those we admire and revere most point us in the direction each of us must go: in the words of the ancient prophet Micah, "to do what is just, to love what is compassionate, and to walk humbly before God."

Printed in the United States
58781LVS00001B/127-150

9 780802 860842